Advance Praise for *Nobody's Child: A Biography*

"Francisque's biography, in a tender, thoughtful way, shines a light on black family life in New York City against the backdrop of her therapy sessions. She captures the family's joy, sorrows, pain and how the convergence of oppression, generational, historical and developmental trauma is upended through resilience and reconciliation. I could not put this book down until I read the entire text... extraordinary!"

-Dr. Juwayriah J. Hassan

"An extremely powerful story of a young woman and the obstacles she faced living this thing we call life. Easy to read, yet kept my interest chapter after chapter. I cried, I prayed, I rejoiced while reading about Brenda from an early age through adulthood. After a few chapters, Brenda became my friend, my sister, my heart. Witnessing her overcome ever obstacle set to destroy and break her was rewarding."

-Katerina D. Sidbury

"I really enjoyed reading the manuscript. It was a very good read (the short chapters were a plus) and the various characters stories weren't difficult to follow. It was a very emotional read and often sad story. However, the individual strength and fortitude of many of the characters was inspirational. Even in of the darkest of behaviors and times there were rays of light."

-Jacob Foster

"Nobody's Child: A Biography is story of generational trauma and how you fall and get up again. The book is a complete surprise of individuals with trauma who pass it along to their children like unpaid debts.

As a biography, the story grips you and reminds you that this is real. It's a story that must be told in order to help other families rise above their defeats."

-Nathasha Parris

"The author examines the typical Black family structure, traditions, beliefs, dynamics, abated truths, appearances, character building, issue resolution and subsequent implications. The story provides the reader with the pervasive socio-ethnic approach to the challenges that are presented.

A carefully crafted account of the characters' lives and their intersection. The similarities and differences are described. The intersection of their lives, encounters and the repercussions provide an intriguing invitation for the next experience. The hardships, struggles, forgiveness, and strength illustrated leaves the reader with a poignant impression of resilience, determination, faith and above all confidence.

Though we may walk through valleys, He never leaves us, He is there to see us through and teach us to trust, believe – and He is there to help reach our victories."

-Darlton E. Haskins

Nobody's Child

A Biography

Tammie Francisque

Copyright © 2020 by Tammie Francisque

All rights are reserved. No part of this publication may be reproduced, stored in a retrieval system or transmitted, in any form or by any means, electronic, mechanical, photocopying, recording or otherwise, without the prior written permission of the publisher.

The Author's Pen, LLC
PO Box 201744
Arlington, Texas 76006
www.tapwriting.com

Publisher's Note: This is a work of non-fiction. This is Brenda's true story; however, some names have been changed to protect the identity of parties who have not given their express permission to share their personal stories.

Nobody's Child: A Biography/ Tammie Francisque. -- 1st ed.
ISBN 978-1-948248-27-3

For Mommy - Because You Matter.

For Daddy – Because You Matter.

And

For Miles and William - for sharing me and loving me so unconditionally.

CONTENTS

ACKNOWLEDGEMENTS

With Humble Thanks:

First and foremost, I would like to thank God. HE has given me the power to believe in my passion and pursue my dreams. I could never have done this without the faith I have in HIM, the Almighty.

To My 'Knight in Shining Armor' - my phenomenal husband, William Francisque, for all of your love, friendship, support, and your high-wire acts with a dollar, thank you from the bottom of my heart... I love you.

To Brenda and Jimmy, two of the strongest, bravest, most loving souls on Earth. I thank you, for giving this book a soul, and for sharing your lives with the world. I love you both.

To Kristell Douglas, Sherry Sigmone and Jewell Sigmone, my big sisters who I love and admire, so glad we have the laughs and the music that's only ours. To the Cole Family, Johnson Family, Wooten Family, Helen Palmer, Gloria Farrell, Pat Ethridge, Vanessa Jenkins-Williams, and my 'uncle' Bobby Jones - Thanks for the seasoning in my stew!

To Dr. Marjorie Kalter, for being the first to tell me I was a great writer, even if you really meant good.

To Dr. Estella Conwill Majozo for showing me the power of female soldiers through literature, and for random acts of kindness.

To Beverly Smith and Lisa Maldonado for true and unlikely friendships. I miss you both.

To my Swaynation, Jamille Mills-DePaz, and ALL my friends, for reading and cheering, and for reminding me that "writers write" and that writing is SEXY. Thank you!

To Juwayriah Hassan, for helping me see how much I matter. You are a warrior!

To my beautiful miracle, Miles, who inspires me each and every day, you are my favorite person in the whole world. Mom loves you more than anything!

To Classic Soul, to R&B, to Old Skool Hip Hop, to Jazz, to Doo Wop, and to All of the Love Songs – for all you've given and continue to give, I treasure you. There will never be anything like you again.

Brenda's eyes stayed fixed on the pastel, distorted images in the abstract Lee Krasner print 'Noon', hanging directly across from the couch she had been lying on for the past hour.

The pink heads with blank expressions, the little brown monkey banging his stick on the silver-trimmed drum, the yellow parakeet with the slanted eyes wearing the brown tam hat to one side. The tiny man in the blue shirt playing a mandolin, and the piglet sporting orange lipstick, yellow dress, and a straw hat, seemingly were on a mission as he pushed his little wagon. She always saw something new in the abstract impressionist piece. These images were like old, familiar friends that made her feel at home in Dr. Juwayriah's office for one hour, twice a week, for the past five years. The piece had been lovingly installed against the south wall of the room. On a day like today, it caught a perfect ray of sun, which unfolded itself across Noon like an expectant lover, complementing and appreciating one last time. Outside, it was a perfect 75 degrees. Another long stream of the sun penetrated the double-paned, lightly tinted glass window while lazy dust particles floated, seemingly suspended, inside the prism of light, finding a temporary home on the caramel-colored parquet floor.

The sun had been a welcome change from the unusual stretch of rainy days in New York City. But, Brenda wasn't complaining. She had never been more grateful for another day to be alive. In a few months, she would celebrate her 63rd birthday. She looked down at her hands, the backsides tannish-brown, barely wrinkled, but now covered with nutmeg-colored freckles that mirrored her mother's lovely hands. It made her smile that she had something of her very own that was inherited.

The single white Kleenex dangling over her head broke her concentration. She reached up and took the tissue from Dr. Juwayriah's hand. She didn't realize she had been crying. "Thanks," she said. The tears were traveling slowly down the left side of her face, over the curves of her ear, and disappeared behind her neck, where she caught them with the tissue. Tears came naturally now; she didn't feel ashamed, but instead, a sense of freedom. She cherished the peacefulness of Dr. Juwayriah's office, so she didn't rush to speak. She knew she didn't have to. Dr. Juwayriah had established long ago that when they reached this point, there would be no rush. At this moment, the memory of the print and reflection of the ray of sunlight would live on forever in her heart.

"It seems like forever ago when I first walked into your office," Brenda said looking over her shoulder at Dr. Juwayriah. "I was broken, lost, confused, and alone" she said. "Five years, two months, three days, four hours, and..." looking at her watch, "...six minutes ago, I came to see you for the very first time." Dr. Juwayriah relaxed back in her chair, placed her tortoise shell pen and pink leather-bound notebook down softly onto the glass and mahogany cocktail table to her left. She was deliberately patient, giving Brenda the time and space she needed for the moment. She did this for all her *graduates*. The strongest ones took the lead on graduation day, confidently guiding the final session, taking their place at the podium, recapping their time at the University. They recalled the ups and downs to show their growth, both to Dr. Juwayriah and themselves. It was empowering, she recognized the dedicated of the graduates. Brenda did the homework by facing the tough challenges. This included reconciling with friends and loved ones. Brenda also forgave colleagues who did not treat her well because they were somewhere between their path toward destruction and the road to recovery. It is this work that Dr. Juwayriah is most proud of because it provides the foundation for building new relationships on their own in post-grad work.

Grads gauge their own readiness by an audit of the overall body of work completed from the first to last session with Dr. Juwayriah. If graduates can conclude their emotional success, it is less likely for them to return for a therapy session. And although she genuinely admired the remarkable woman before her, she <u>did not</u> want to see her on the couch ever again.

"Do you remember the first thing I ever said to you, Dr. Juwayriah?" asked Brenda. "Yes," said the doctor. "You asked, rather loudly, "What in the hell is wrong with me?!!" Brenda managed a smile, shaking her head at the thought. She fumbled with the tissue in her hands, still damp with her tears, and allowed herself to go back in time. She had forgiven her younger self long ago, back when she didn't love herself as much as she did now. She had seen a lot, and done even more. After a long pause, she said, "I am blessed, and I know my life is worth remembering."

Dr. Juwayriah: "Tell Me About Your Dad."

Brenda: "Dad was rough. He really didn't give me the time of day. And, as a little girl, that hurt my feelings so much. His very presence affected me in ways that I can only now understand. But, back then I loved him and hated him all at the same time.

Chapter One

Coral Garrett Hill had little time for long, motherly hugs and bedtime stories. She had five children by the age of 24, and a husband who worked two full-time jobs to keep food on the table. Her second child, Wilbert Hill (everyone called him 'Dill') learned to take care of his own needs as well as the needs of his three younger sisters, Maggie, Catherine ('Kate'), and Joanie at a very young age. By 1923, when he was nine and his big brother Charlie was eleven, they earned money by delivering fresh fruit from the farmer's market to elderly church ladies who could no longer go out and shop. The ladies would still bake pies and scratch cakes 'for the Lord', and the boys would carefully deliver them to church before service started. The boys pooled the little money they earned together to help with household expenses and even pick up little trinkets for their younger sisters. Coral had taught her boys the importance of treating women with kindness and respect, and most of all the value of working hard to taking care of family. When Dill was thirteen years old, she told him, "In a few years, you'll find a nice. clean girl to marry and care of home, just like your daddy, ya hear?" "Yes, Ma'am," he'd say.

"Family is the only thing that matters," said Coral.

Coral's husband Edmund was a stern man with a kind heart who loved

his family and worked since the age of 12. He would come home in the

middle of the night between jobs to eat a meal that Coral would keep

warm for him. In the morning when Coral and the children would wake

up, Edmund would already be at work. The kids rarely saw their father.

Edmund missed most of Dill's childhood. Dill respected how hard his

father worked, yet resented not having him around.

Dill had made up his mind that he was not going to be a factory

worker like his father. He was going to be a fighter pilot in the U.S. Air

Force as soon as he got old enough to enlist, just like his hero Eugene

Jacques Bullard. Bullard was the first Negro fighter pilot to serve in the

U.S. Air Force. He also fought in World War I. He had seen pictures of

Bullard as a child, and admired how strong and tall he stood as he posed

in the photo beside his airplane. Dill thought he would make history too,

by becoming the first colored fighter pilot from his small hometown of

Willow Grove, Pennsylvania.

By the time Dill was 16, he stood 5'10", and had a slim but fit,

muscular build. His perfectly straight white teeth brought out his light honey colored skin and sandy light-brown hair. Although he had the interest of many girls in his town, Dill had his eyes on a particular girl he met while working a summer job with his brother Charlie. His brother Charlie had married his sweetheart Tina a year earlier, and the newlyweds secured jobs as chauffer and maid for the Van Hoortens, a wealthy white family in Westchester, NY. Charlie reasoned this would give him and Tina an opportunity to live in a beautiful guesthouse, and be together, while building their nest egg to purchase their own home someday. Dill had run errands for the family the previous summer. The Van Hoortens knew and thought highly of him. So, when they required an additional chauffer, Charlie suggested Dill.

> *Juwayriah: "Let's Talk About Your Mom now."*
>
> *Brenda: (Sigh).... Mom was an Angel. She was the kindest, softest person you could meet. But, she was tough too... just like her brothers... She seemed so different from me, even though people said I looked just like her, for the most part. I loved her, I still do.*

The Daniels

Alice Georgina Daniels was the second of eleven children born to Maria and George Daniels. She was a fair-skinned beauty with rosy lips and cheeks, soft brown eyes and shy smile. The few light brown freckles across her nose and cheeks made her face even more attractive. Dill was immediately taken with her beauty and innocence. She was exactly the kind of girl his mom would approve of for him.

The Daniels family lived in one of the five homes on Grove Hill Lane in the town of Penn Lynn, Pennsylvania. Penn Lynn was just fifteen minutes east of Willow Grove once you crossed over the railroad tracks.

In 1916, when the Daniels came to Grove Hill Lane, there were only dirt roads and tall stalks of wheat congregating and leaning over each carved-out section of land where homes were built. Large, round stones and boulders were positioned from the open dirt road up to the front porches of houses to create a walkway and to separate the properties. There were no streetlights in Penn Lynn so everyone stayed indoors after dark. The only light that could be seen outside in the evenings were lights from passing trains on the railroad that ran behind the homes.

Alice, born that same year, was raised Catholic and attended bible school and church on Sundays with her family. Any free time was spent caring for her younger siblings, or reading. She loved reading poetry, her favorites being 'To Maecenas' and 'On Being Brought from Africa to America' both by Phyllis Wheatley, and the works of poet Claude McKay. And although her studies and family duties didn't leave her much free time, what she longed for most was to be an accomplished painter. She read everything she could about the great Impressionists Monet and Renoir. But, what she was most inspired by was the bold rebellion of Fauvism by Andre Derain and Henri Matise. She decided she wasn't going to live and die in Pennsylvania. She was going to college, and she would study art history, maybe become an art teacher. She knew her parents couldn't afford to send her to college. Therefore, she planned to earn as much money as possible to pay for her own education, then work her way through school, whatever it took.

After completing secondary school, she secured a job as a domestic working for a wealthy family in Westchester, NY. Alice had only been working there for a short time when a handsome Dill Hill arrived on the estate and began working as one of two chauffeurs for the Van Hoorten family.

It took a while, but Dill finally worked up the courage to ask Alice out on a date. It took three tries before she said yes, and they began dating. Alice shared her dreams of becoming an art teacher and a famous painter, and Dill shared his aspirations of becoming a fighter pilot. When Alice took Dill home to meet her family most everyone thought he was a handsome, respectable, and quite the conscientious gentleman, except for Alice's sisters. They were suspicious of him because they had heard he had lots of ladies. They were overprotective of their big sister. But, Alice was becoming quite fond of Dill, and continued dating him anyway. She had already known Charlie and Tina, and enjoyed spending time with Dill's sisters and brother. She and everyone else knew, even at that time that Alice loved Dill, and she would marry him whenever he asked.

Dill had fallen in love with Alice, as well. But, he was not thinking about marriage just yet. He was more focused on fulfilling his Air Force dreams. He hadn't yet received his assignment on where he would have to report, and he was becoming concerned. He visited the recruiting station where his paperwork was to be processed, and was finally advised that his application had been rejected for 'unknown' reasons. When he inquired further about what happened, the recruiter who interviewed him said "You BOYS ain't built to fly. You better fit for pickin' cotton." Dill was crushed. He had been warned by nearly everyone that this could happen. It didn't matter how much he learned or how hard he worked, it was his skin color that held him back and he resented that deeply. In the end, Dill grudgingly joined the Army, like his father and brother before him, and served three years while Alice waited for him.

While Dill was completing his tour of duty, Alice had taken a second job as a nurses' aide at the Berch Crescent Medical Facility. She fed and changed the premature babies, and assisted new mothers with post-labor care. She was always good at her job as well as taking care of her sisters and brothers. Alice was a natural. But, with this job she got to interact with the mothers and talk with them about what it was like to be pregnant, give birth and be married. She didn't want to compromise on her academic dreams, but she also didn't want to lose Dill.

On August 12, 1938, 22-year-old Alice married 24-year-old Dill in a small ceremony in front of their families, and very few friends. Alice's sisters clapped reluctantly with worried smiles, as the vows were completed. They gave one another a familiar look as the new Mr. and Mrs. Wilbert Hill greeted their guests. Alice smiled a joyous smile, and locked into the loving embrace of her new husband.

Batter Up!

The newlyweds moved into a small, one-bedroom apartment in Brooklyn, NY. Dill secured a job with Metro Bus Lines as a bus driver. He worked the 8am to 4pm shift on the Essex Line, and Alice continued to work the domestic job that was closer to her home. One year later, Alice gave birth to her first child, Norman. Less than a year later she gave birth to baby girl, Marilyn. Alice was forced to quit her job and give her full attention to caring for her husband, her home and her two beautiful babies.

By the time the kids were 4 and 5 years old, Dill began drinking more regularly. He was stopping off at the neighborhood pub, and hanging with his buddies for two hours instead of going straight home after work. He confided in his friends and sulked into his whiskey glass, "I wasn't supposed to be just a bus driver, or just a husband, or just a father... I could have been so much more..." His buddies, who were blue collar workers themselves, did not take offense. They understood what he meant. They too had big dreams growing up that didn't quite work out the way they had planned.

Alice tried to reassure Dill about how valuable he was to their family, and told him how proud of him she was. But, it didn't matter much to Dill. Instead, he pushed Alice away, and cut her off emotionally and intimately. Alice became a lonely mother of two. And now, although Dill was rarely home, she was pregnant with their third child. Alice was sad that Dill had turned into a different man in such a short time. Her sisters rallied around her and visited from Pennsylvania to help out with the children, and to just keep Alice company.

Eight months into Alice's third pregnancy, Dill came home drunk in a jealous rage. He immediately noticed a dirty dish and cup sitting on the table. He huffed and threw down his keys, took off his jacket, turned on the television, and plopped down in his chair. Alice, already on her way to bring an ice cold can of beer and snacks, noticed him looking at the table and immediately rushed over to grab the dish and cup to take it into the kitchen. "I work all day and you can't even clean up the house?!" he shot at her. Alice had intended to clear away the dishes and have them washed before Dill reached home, but, she had been cleaning the kids' room and washing clothes all day. She quickly washed the dish and cup, and was about to go upstairs to finish folding the laundry when she felt Dill walking closely behind her. She paused to let him pass, thinking he wanted to go upstairs, but he just stood there scowling at her. She nervously walked up the stairs in front of him, carefully holding herself underneath her belly. When she reached the top of the steps, she turned and saw Dill leaning on the wall at the bottom, continuing to stare while drinking his beer.

There was something in the way he looked at her, as if he couldn't stand the sight of her. He didn't say a word. He continued to observe her with a piercing stare. She went into the bedroom, leaving the door slightly ajar. After folding the clothes, she balanced them on her left arm and opened the door wide to take them downstairs to the linen closet. The house was eerily quiet with the exception of the television playing downstairs. Dill didn't appear to be anywhere in sight. Just as she reached the edge of the staircase, she felt a heavy shove from behind. Alice tumbled face-first down the flight of stairs. At the bottom of the landing she lay twisted, crying and screaming in excruciating pain, begging for her husband to help her. Dill calmly made his way downstairs, stepped over Alice, and picked up the phone. "Nita, come get your sister and take her to the hospital. She just fell down the stairs."

Despite his wife's cries for help, he walked into the kitchen, grabbed another ice cold beer out of the refrigerator, sat down in his chair and watched television. He refused to answer the door when Anita arrived, forcing Alice to struggle to her feet. Somehow she managed to open the door, collapsing into her sister's arms. Alice's condition took priority over anything Anita wanted to say to Dill. So, without a word, she rushed her sister to the hospital for emergency care. Alice was admitted immediately, and treated for a fractured cheekbone, dislocated left shoulder, and a badly bruised left hip. She was also treated for dehydration and exhaustion. The doctors said it was a miracle the baby survived under such duress. She was hospitalized for the whole ninth month of her pregnancy, and Alice was happy for the break. Anita, along with Alice's 18-year-old sister Janie who came home from college, stayed with the family while Alice recuperated.

On the rare occasions when Dill would lay off the drinking, Janie could actually tolerate Dill. He would be looking pitiful sitting at the dining room table reading the paper and snacking on walnuts and cold coffee. She would feel sorry for him, and offer to make him a sandwich or make a fresh pot of coffee. He would give her a grateful half smile. It was during these times that Janie thought Dill wasn't a total monster. There was a glimmer of hope that her sister wasn't completely out of her mind for marrying such a man.

One sweltering July afternoon, Janie was doing her chores while the kids were playing outside. She was compiling a grocery list, when Dill offered to drive her to the store. Dill had never offered to do anything nice for her throughout the time that she had known him. Usually, he pretended to be completely unaware that she could benefit from his assistance. She would struggle on the bus with grocery bags, taking nearly an hour to get back home to prepare a meal in time for dinner. She really didn't want to take any charity from Dill. However, given the weather and long morning she already had, she decided to go against her better judgment and she accepted his offer. On the way, Dill made idle chatter about Janie's college campus, her studies, and the weather. Janie cautiously answered the questions, but gradually relaxed and actually, for once, enjoyed the company of her brother-in-law. Once they arrived, Dill parked the car and then pulled his silk-banned brown hat down over his eyes as he reclined the front seat to catch a nap while Janie shopped. When she returned with the groceries, he drove her back to the house, offering to help prepare the meal. Janie couldn't believe his sudden transformation. After dinner, Janie tucked in the kids for the night, while Dill wedged his fully satisfied belly down into the curve of his favorite chair and took in a little TV. Impressed by his behavior, Janie went out of her way to stop by the living room to tell him goodnight with a warm and friendly smile. He replied in kind, then popped open one of two cold cans of beer that were already sweating along with Dill. As Janie turned to walk toward the bedroom, Dill stared at her tight, shapely body between the edges of her robe. "Sleep tight." he said, only loud enough for himself to hear.

A few hours and three beers later, Dill could not get the picture of Janie's body out of his mind. He crept down the hallway toward the bedrooms, and listened quietly with his ear to Janie's door. He heard only silence. He opened the door slowly, and saw Janie sprawled across the bed, her nightgown halfway up her left thigh. Dill slipped in the room and closed the door behind him. Janie was startled awake by Dill's hot, alcohol-laced breath on the back of her neck. She could feel his hard penis rubbing into the crease of her ass through her white cotton nightgown. For a second, she froze in a panic as she realized that she was trapped between the wall and her brother-in-law. She wriggled herself towards the headboard, hoping to get leverage so she could turn and face her attacker. Dill managed to squeeze his hand under her body, grabbing her left breast and pulled her body closer to him. He moved his left hand under the sheet and up her left thigh to the top band of her silk panties and groaned. She attempted to scream, but Dill rolled her onto her stomach. With most of his weight pressing down on her back, she could barely breathe, much less scream. Despite her best defenses, Dill managed to lower her panties to below the curves of her ass. She realized that if she didn't stop him soon, he would take what she had never given to any man. Janie pulled his right hand up from her breast and bit down as hard as she could just below his wrist. Dill screamed out in pain as her teeth tore through his flesh. "Dammit, woman. You bit me!!!"

Janie broke free from Dill's grasp and grabbed the wooden bat she kept at the side of the nightstand just in case. She stepped back raising the bat like a professional baseball player. A part of her hoped that he would step up to the plate. But, another part of her was slightly scared that he would try to kill her, given his much bigger size. But, right now she felt anger more than any other emotion. She spat out Dill's blood and flesh she had ripped from his hand onto the floor. Gritting through clenched bloody teeth and seething rage, she yelled "Get the hell out of here, you drunken fool! I knew I shouldn't have trusted you." Dill rose up from the bed, wincing and holding his hand, dripping blood on the pale blue carpet. Before he left the room, he took note of Janie in her white nightgown standing in a batter's stance across the room. Despite the pain, he was aroused by her feistiness. She didn't realize it, but he could see her every curve as her silhouette stood out against the moon's glow. 'Thank God for moonlight", he muttered to himself. As he headed down the hall, he heard the door slam shut then lock. In the bathroom he cleaned and bandaged his arm. He knew better than to try anything like that again with Janie. He had paid the price in blood this time, and he decided it wasn't worth it. A second attempt could cost him his life.

For the remainder of time Alice was hospitalized, Janie and Dill did not speak. She moved around him, and he avoided her. This suited Janie just fine. As long as he stayed in his place, she would not have to kill her sister's husband. To be safe, Dill made it a point not to drink or eat any food Janie prepared for fear she'd poison him. Neither one of them ever spoke a word of the incident to anyone.

Betrayal & Sacrifice

Brenda: "The hardest part was the silence… and the darkness."

When Dill arrived to Queens General Hospital on August 22, 1942, twenty-six-year-old Alice had given birth to her third child and named her Brenda. Brenda was a carbon copy of her mother, only four shades darker. As a matter of fact, she was darker than everyone in the family, with the exception of Norman, who was only a half-hue lighter. Actually, Norman had been the darkest person in the family up until then, with Dill, Alice and Marilyn all being what is referred to as 'redbone.' But, alas, Norman was lucky enough to be born a boy. And as long as Dill had a son to carry on his name, he didn't seem to mind what color he was.

Peering through the glass and seeing Brenda's tiny pecan brown hand clutched around Alice's finger gave Dill the sinking feeling he had almost willed into existence. He didn't want it to be true, but he was absolutely certain, in his gut, that this baby was not of his blood. He entered into his wife's hospital room without saying a word. He walked around the hospital bassinet, bile rising in his belly as he pretended not to see his family name "HILL" in bold black letters at the foot of the bassinet. Alice looked beautiful, radiant. He did love her so much. She watched him with nothing but love and longing in her eyes. "Her name is Brenda... Isn't she beautiful?" she asked, reaching out for the baby's tiny hand. He looked at this brown baby, with absolutely none of HIS features, and could feel his face getting hot. His eyes went cold. Alice's face turned sad, and then immediately scared. She reached for her baby, picked her up quickly and held her close to her chest, covering her tiny face. The silence was deafening. The baby began to fuss. Alice rocked her baby softly, never taking her eyes off her husband's face. Dill backed away from the bed... and from his wife. He stood with his back to the window, a heated mixture of anger and disgust filling him. He had only been there for fifteen minutes, but it felt like a lifetime. He needed a drink. He walked over to his wife, leaned down very close to her face, and lingered there. Her heart was beating out of her chest now. She could feel his warm breath on her cheek and then her ear. In a voice she knew too well of late, he low growled "That...thing... is not mine." He stood up, glared at her and the baby, and left the room.

Brokenhearted, and in tears, Alice was slowly coming to grips with the reality that her new baby's fate was an uncertain one. She was a housewife with no resources of her own, and two other children to care for. She stared at her baby, cried, and pulled her close to her chest. She used this time away from Dill to bond with Brenda. She knew it was going to be a rough road ahead for both of them, but she was determined to protect her new baby from Dill.

Dill was not the most caring or sensitive father to his children. He didn't show affection openly, and wasn't vocal about his feelings toward his children. He didn't concern himself with his children's development, well-being or social activities. That was Alice's job as far as he was concerned. Like his father, he was primarily a financial provider for his family. He was hardly ever home and rarely visited Alice while she was in the hospital (and would only enter the room if baby Brenda was out in the nursery.) He worked long hours. And, when he wasn't at work, he was drinking with his friends at the neighborhood pub.

Once Alice and Brenda were home from the hospital, Alice tried her best to get back into her demanding domestic roles of mother and wife. Janie helped with the baby whenever she could. But, she had a full course load and couldn't be there as much as before. Dill stayed away from the house more and more. But, when he was at home, he did not make things easy. Dill refused to allow Alice to bring Brenda to the dinner table with the rest of the family. Alice would have to feed the

newborn in her crib, and then come down to eat dinner with Dill, Norman

and Marilyn. Afterwards, Alice would have to clean the dinner dishes

and wipe down the kitchen while Dill sat in his chair directly across from

the television, drinking until he fell asleep. He demanded that Alice keep

HER daughter out of his presence at all times. He resented that the baby

was even there in his house. It was as if the very sight of her filled his

mind with random scenes of another man making love to his wife. Dill

felt that the child was a living reminder that at one point, another man

had been given what was rightfully his under God. Deep inside, he knew

the child was innocent. But, his ego would not let Alice's betrayal go

unpunished. His heart had been broken once again, and the pain would

likely never fade.

By the time Brenda was six months old Dill had enough. He called

his sister and asked her to come over for a visit. He confided in her

"Katey…. it's not mine. I won't raise it." His face was stern and sincere.

"I want you and Dave to take her." A look of shock and surprise crossed

her face. She was trying to process what her brother was saying. His

wife had just given birth to her third child. Did he expect for her to just

give up her baby? She never would, she thought. Kate, unable to have

a child of her own, knew she could never give her child away if she were

Alice, but the thought of her becoming a mother interested her. But, then she thought of Dave. Dave loved children. But, Dave would not want to raise Dill and Alice's child. He didn't care who the 'real' father was, he believed the baby was innocent and it was Dill's responsibility to raise her. She knew Dave loved her, and would certainly wish her happiness. But, there was no way Dave would go for this one. Sitting across from her brother in that living room, Kate quickly weighed the options. She would most certainly catch hell when she got home, but her thinking was 'When I walk in with the baby, he won't be able to say no.' And besides, right now, she really didn't care what Dave wanted. She had decided, right then, that she would take the baby, and raise her. Dave could be a part of it, or not.

Dill interrupted her thoughts, "If you don't take her, Katey... I'll give her away to someone else. I really don't care," he said calmly. "What about Alice?" Dill snapped, "WHAT ABOUT HER??!! SHE'S THE ONE...." He stopped himself. He couldn't even say it out loud. It was too painful.

Life with Kate & Dave

Kate and Dave met in the town of Penn Lynn, Pennsylvania. Dave courted her for three years before they were married on June 9, 1939. In December 1940, Kate miscarried a baby boy in her first trimester, and was advised by her doctor that she would never be strong enough to bear children. This was a devastating blow to Kate and Dave, who both wanted to have a big family like the ones they both had grown up in. Dave never wanted to discuss the loss of the baby, and Kate decided to bury it deep down inside and throw herself into her missionary work and lab technician job for which she was formally trained. She secured a position at Columbia University where she assisted research scientists in finding a cure for contagious diseases from campylobacteriosis to the common cold. She was extremely proud of the work she was doing, because she felt she was contributing something good to the world. Kate was a devout woman who listened to gospel music and took much pride in caring for her family. She was a kind woman with a good heart, but she was also stern and ran a 'tight ship' at home.

Dave was a truck driver for Allied Moving Van Company. He was a tall, fairly quiet man who worked hard and provided a good home for his wife. He loved to read the newspaper, watch television, play pinochle, poker and solitaire, smoke lots of cigarettes, drink Scotch, and cuss. He'd spend time doing all of these things alone or with friends and family. He enjoyed entertaining in his home, as did Kate.

He was very stern where Brenda was concerned and showed little affection or tenderness openly. He loved her in his own way, but could also be harsh with his words if she was disobedient or behaved badly (which wasn't often). He would tell her "Do the right thing" instead of offering tender words of encouragement. He and Kate could both be excessively harsh with their words when annoyed with something Brenda did. One afternoon when Brenda had been out riding her bike for hours, she pulled the bike into the driveway on the side of the house and laid it down partly blocking the way for their landlady, Mrs. Johnson's car to pull in. She would have laid it against the wall of the house as she had been previously instructed to do, but she had to pee and couldn't hold it. She ran into the house, heading upstairs taking two steps at a time and simultaneously unbuttoning her beige capris on the way. She quickly relieved herself, washed her hands and face, then she headed back downstairs to take care of the bicycle. But, before she could reach

the bottom step Dave, who had been sitting in his favorite lounge chair

in the den, was on her "Didn't I tell you a thousand times not to leave

your bike lying in the driveway?! What are you, stupid or somethin'?"

It was a rhetorical question, and usually didn't require a response. She

stood there fingering the trim of her white shirt, looking down at her

scuffed black and white shoes with the red marshmallow soles, using her

left toe to dust the road dirt off of the now gray sock on her right ankle.

"Did you hear what I said, girl?" "Yes, Sir" she replied quickly. He

rolled his eyes, then flipped the evening newspaper back into place and

went back to reading. She slowly eased out of the den and out the front

door to tend to the bike. Being called 'stupid' or 'fool' was a regular

part of Kate and Dave's vocabulary when it came to Brenda and sadly,

she had become used to it. She always received good grades, was

generally well-behaved, and did her best to be helpful around the house,

but it did hurt her feelings when they called her names. She tried not to

take it personally, because even as a child she realized she was fortunate

to have them as parents. But, it was hurtful nonetheless. She believed

they loved her in their own special way. She was, after all, their relative,

and just a small child. She often wondered if they spoke to her this way because she wasn't their real daughter. Or, for Dave, maybe because she wasn't a boy.

Dave enjoyed working with his hands, often taking on big and small outdoor projects like building a shed, re-sodding the lawn, pulling weeds, whatever needed to be done. He would recruit Brenda and some of the boys in the neighborhood as his students and show them how to fix things or let them participate in small building projects like birdhouses and mailboxes. After spending many years in the moving and trucking industry, Dave knew everything there was to know about the moving business. Occasionally, he would take Brenda with him out on moving jobs, and she would help with lamps and other small items. When moving large pieces like refrigerators, Dave would call Brenda over "Now, when you move a refrigerator, you have to put it on a '45 to clear the ceiling." That meant it had to be leaned over on its side at a 45-degree angle in order for it to get up the stairs and not scrape the ceiling. He taught her how to measure a doorway with a tape measure and with her eyes. Dave would say "Learn to work well with your hands, Brenda, and you will always be able to find a job." Brenda not only enjoyed having father-daughter time with Dave, but she also loved to work with her hands. It was something she was naturally good at, and Dave called her a "quick learner."

Still, there were a few moments when Brenda felt a little tenderness from Dave. He would squeeze Brenda between him and the other two men on his moving crew in the front seat of the huge moving truck. Brenda would sit wide-eyed as she pretended not to be listening to the men talk freely about women's breasts, and their sexual exploits. Dave would clear his throat and remind them often that there was "a lady present." They would apologize to Brenda, and then Dave would give her a wink, which meant it was their little secret. If Kate knew the men were using filthy, un-Godly language around her, she would never let her go to work with Dave again.

Dave had very few buddies. He worked with a lot of white men, and some of them he even spent time with outside of work. The handful of black men he did hang around were part of his immediate circle, being members of either his or Kate's family. Dave's boss, Mr. Altonelli was one of the few white men Dave respected and thought of highly. Mr. Altonelli admired Dave's work ethic. He treated him as an equal and openly displayed his friendship toward Dave, even in the presence of his white employees, which was considered dangerous behavior in Flatbush, Brooklyn in 1950. Mr. Altonelli visited the Robinson home on special occasions and discussed politics over cigars and warm brandy. He always got to leave with a warm, homemade apple pie baked especially for him by Kate.

Christmas time in the Robinson house was always a special time. Kate and Dave always went out of their way to get into the holiday spirit. They would sneak out weeks before Christmas to get gifts for Brenda and other family members. For years, they would hide the wrapped presents deep in the back of the basement storage closet behind the laundry room, until Brenda figured out the hiding spot and discovered the presents. Until that time, Kate had always baked fresh cookies and left them on the coffee table with a glass of milk for Santa. The family ritual was two days before Christmas, Dave would decorate the entire outside of the house, roof, bushes and fence. The night before Christmas is when Dave would put up the tree, and allow Brenda to help decorate it with pretty lights, bulbs, garland, and Kate's vintage angel figurines. Kate would make a kitchen full of food including baked macaroni and cheese, yams with toasted marshmallows, collard greens, baked honey-glazed ham with pineapple on top, roast beef, turkey with dressing, cranberry sauce, corn bread stuffing, and all different kinds of fruit pies and cakes. Kate also made her famous homemade cider, which was one of Brenda's favorite holiday treats.

One Christmas, as a small child, Brenda wanted something extra special from Santa Claus. She had pictures of the pristine green and white Cadillac Schwinn truck bicycle cut out and taped onto the wall across from her bed. It was a western-themed bike, and she loved to pretend she was Hop-Along Cassidy, a blond-haired white cowboy who wore an all-black outfit and rode a white horse. Every morning for months before Christmas she would open her eyes and get excited that Santa might bring it to her, if she was good. On Christmas morning Brenda ran downstairs to the living room and beside the tree was the Cadillac Schwinn sitting in front of the tree with a huge red ribbon tied on top of it. No one in her neighborhood had a Cadillac Schwinn, and she would be the envy of her friends. Brenda was so excited. She loved that bike so much, she pulled it into her bedroom and slept with her hand across it. She took pride in caring for the bike and took on extra chores like emptying the garbage, and worked odd jobs for neighbors to earn money to buy upgrades for the bike. Sometimes she got an extra fifty cents and she was elated. She earned enough to buy black and white saddle bags for the sides of the seat, and a shiny silver light for the front of the bike. Shortly after Christmas, Dave came home holding a medium sized box wrapped in brown paper. He handed it to Brenda and she giddily tore at the paper. Inside was a black cowboy outfit, complete with western shirt, black denim stitched pants, black plastic cowboy boots with gold painted spurs, two plastic holsters, two toy six-shooters, and a black felt cowboy hat. Brenda screamed with joy, and ran up to her room to try on her outfit. She admired herself in the mirror, checking herself out from the tip of her hat to the spurs on her heels. She looked like a real life cowboy. Yee-Haw! She wore the outfit every chance she got, and even wore it outside in 20-degree weather. When Kate protested, Brenda said, "But, I want to show it to my friends." Kate told her "You're going to freeze your tail off." But Brenda did not care.

Although Kate treated Brenda as her own daughter, she always made it clear to her that Alice and Dill were her real parents, and that she was a 'Hill' same as her sister Marilyn and brother Norman. Kate and Dave had never legally adopted Brenda, so her last name remained as it was on her birth certificate, "Hill". As a Christian woman, she encouraged a good relationship between Brenda and her birth parents, but also with her siblings. So, she took Brenda to visit the Hill house when she could, so that way, she would know her true, immediate family in a more personal way (as opposed to only interacting when the entire family gathered for weddings and funerals).

Dill kept up his end of the agreement, allowing these visits and keeping his distance, but not without brooding about it. Frankly, he didn't care what the terms were, as long as he didn't have to raise Brenda. When she would come to the house, he would keep quiet, pretend to be completely immersed in the television or crossword puzzle or newspaper article. Once Brenda was gone, then everything could go back to normal. He could keep pretending she didn't exist, or at the very least, that she was a distant related niece with no connection to him at all.

Kate overcompensated for Dill's shortcomings by creating what she believed to be a normal, happy environment for any respectable Christian young lady. There was lots of love. But, where their home may have been lacking in long, warm embraces, it provided all of the things Kate deemed as necessary.

Brenda had her own room, pretty clothes, and, at least on the surface, was a happy child. She attended Public School 181, was outgoing and sociable, and had friends on Lott Street where they lived. Brenda loved Kate and Dave, and gladly called them mom and dad. She longed for a connection with her birth parents, but loved that she could be normal in her life with Kate and Dave.

Kate was very guarded and overprotective of Brenda. She was never comfortable with leaving Brenda at anyone's house while she shopped or ran errands, and especially not overnight. Not even with family members. There had been too many stories about little girls being touched by an uncle or a friend of the family when not closely supervised, and Kate refused to allow that to happen to Brenda. So, she would take her practically everywhere she went: grocery shopping, visiting friends, cocktail parties, church services, evening social functions, anywhere she went.

Kate was a faithful member of Mt. Zion AME Church in Brooklyn, so as a result Brenda spent a lot of time there. Kate was a great singer and was often a featured soloist with the choir. Brenda loved to watch and hear Kate sing. When Kate realized 8-year-old Brenda could also sing, she enrolled her in the junior choir. Ms. Hale, the choir director, would play the piano beautifully, leading all the children in lengthy church productions of stories from the Bible. When Brenda was granted the role of the Angel in Mt. Zion's production of 'Get Semit to Calvary', she was extremely proud, and so was Kate. They would practice for hours at home because Kate wanted to make sure Brenda got her songs and lines just right. Brenda was elated that her mother was proud of her talents and hard work. Ministering in song provided a connection, a platform for Brenda to 'talk' to Kate about something she was passionate about, the Lord. When they practiced and raised their voices toward God, and Kate beamed with pride, Brenda felt close to Kate. She felt loved and valuable. She pleased her mother greatly. She wanted to hold onto that feeling forever.

Kate was a notable baker. She made all kinds of fresh fruit pies, scratch cakes, deep-dish casseroles, and homemade biscuits for the church. Brenda would always ask Kate to teach her to bake from scratch. But Kate didn't like anyone messing around in her kitchen. She treated it as her private space, and the only thing Brenda was allowed to do in there was wash and put away dishes. If anybody wanted something out of the kitchen, Kate would go and get it for them. It was always kept spotless and stocked with food and goodies that were off limits without permission. That's the way Kate liked it, and everyone respected her space. In some strange way, the kitchen became a source of contention for Brenda. Oddly, it was the one place in the house where Brenda could not 'reach' Kate. There were too many rules there, like a museum where nothing could be moved out of place without an alarm sounding and the police showing up to cart the apple cobbler bandit off to jail.

Tomboys & Tiramisu

Growing up in a home without siblings, Brenda developed a sense of loneliness that didn't match her friendly, bubbly persona out in public. All of her friends had sisters, brothers and cousins who lived with them or lived nearby. This disconnect in her life left a void she couldn't quite describe. She had so many questions about her birth parents, as well as her siblings, but didn't dare ask Kate or Dave. The topic was off limits. She wanted Kate to explain, even give a promise of future disclosure. But, Kate dismissed any explanation, with her eyes and body language. She became visibly anxious, busied herself if any friends or other visiting family members would tread on the subject of babies, cheating, or skin color dichotomies. Kate was sad, and Dave was mad. Huffing, puffing, hmpfs, and steely glares, all in Kate's direction. Knowing looks, but never did any words follow.

Brenda busied herself with listening to radio programs or doo-wop records. Sometimes she would go down into the basement and create her own fun using props and her imagination. She'd dress up in cowboy outfits and decorate the entire basement in a country/western theme, or she would get into her make-believe car and drive off to somewhere exotic. Other times, she acted out romantic scenes and she'd play all of the parts. She enjoyed finding different ways to entertain herself. It gave her an opportunity to pretend to be someone else, living someone else's life. It became a way of escaping reality.

Around the neighborhood, Brenda was quite popular. She didn't care much for jumping rope, hopscotch or playing with dolls. She preferred outdoor games with the boys, like running, sweating, tackling, climbing, and getting very dirty... much to Kate's chagrin. Brenda was always picked first for stickball, because she could really whack a ball way into the outfield with a tiny broomstick. Dave always chuckled when Brenda would come home and describe the look on the boys' faces when she did so. He called her "little Jackie Robinson" and said she was a natural.

The only time Brenda liked playing with doll houses and girl toys was when she visited her friends from school, Rose Guccione and Annette Carbonera. Rose and Annette were two Italian girls from Brenda's class at P.S. 181. They lived across Rogers and New York Avenues, around the corner from where Dave worked.

All the black kids in the neighborhood were told repeatedly by their parents <u>not</u> to cross over New York Avenue. It was understood that the white gangs (who resembled the boys in the movie Grease) would chase and beat up any black kids who crossed the line, boy or girl. Brenda didn't understand why she couldn't just go play with her friends and snuck over there anyway. Occasionally, if a kid saw Brenda take off on her bike in the wrong direction, they would shout after her "Whitey lover" and "Where you goin', whitey-lover?" She would shout back over her shoulder "Mind your own damn business!" and kept pedaling as fast as she could.

Sherm, one of the tallest boys in her neighborhood, would stand in front of Brenda's bike to prevent her from moving, that is if he could catch her. She'd stare him down and then lay her bike down slowly, keeping her eyes on him. Next thing you know there would be punching, slapping and kicking from every direction. Afterwards, she would look a mess with hair torn out of her box braids, ripped shirt and stained pants. She was always careful not to let anyone get close to her face, because she knew she wouldn't be able to hide the scars from Kate and Dave. She always kept her fists up and leaned in the way Dave had taught her when she was 7 years old. Boys usually punched her in the arms and legs, but girls fought dirty. They always went straight for the face, pulled hair and tore clothes.

After a fight, she would sneak back into the house to clean up before Kate or Dave could see she'd been in a fight. She knew she would have to explain why she was fighting, and then she wouldn't be able to sneak across Rogers anymore. She wasn't about to let that happen.

On the days she would make it over to Rose and Annette's without incident, it would usually be a good day. She would leave her bike parked around the corner from Dave's job so no one would recognize her and walk over to her friends' apartment buildings. Four 8-story red brick buildings surrounded the courtyard, and in the center sat a large, circular water fountain with a statue of a chubby, naked boy reaching one hand upward toward the sky. Rose lived in building A and Annette lived in building C. Rose and Annette treated Brenda like a 'true' friend, not like their black friend. Annette's mom was a fantastic baker like Kate, and always offered the girls homemade Italian desserts like Pastaciatti, Torrone and Tiramisu. She would call the girls to the kitchen table to sample the treats, and even invited Brenda for sleepovers. Kate wouldn't permit sleepovers, but because she did like Annette's parents and she occasionally would allow Brenda to go for ice cream with the family.

One day, after leaving Annette's, Brenda and Rose walked around the corner to get Brenda's bike. Once there, a couple of white boys standing nearby called Rose a "nigger lover." Rose began to argue with them, then went over to them and said something that Brenda could not hear. Afterwards, she came back over to Brenda, smiled and said she would see her at school. Brenda did not ask what she had said to them. The next time Brenda visited and saw those same boys, they turned around and walked away without saying a word. She wasn't sure what Rose said to them, but they never bothered her again. Years later she learned that Rose's dad was the owner of a large plastic manufacturing company, and was very influential on the east coast. One of the bully's father worked for her dad, and she had threatened to have her father not only fire the man but blackball him should he ever bother her or Brenda again.

Bullies & Butterflies

Georgie Anderson was an ashy-brown-skinned boy with a reddish-brown short haircut. His big ears contrasted his oblong head and his full bottom lip hung low to reveal a sprinkling of brown and pink gums under his bottom row of teeth. Georgie lived on Lott Street, a few houses down from Kate's friend Mrs. Cambridge. When Brenda went for a visit Georgie was always there to greet her. "Hi, Brenda, you look niiiice today." Brenda would roll her eyes (when Kate wasn't nearby) and suck her teeth and tell him, "Shut up, stupid." Georgie's lip would poke out more and in his high-pitched voice he'd respond "I was just tryin' to be nice, you ole ugly girl. Forget 'choo then." He would ride off on his bike or kick a can down the street toward his house. Brenda knew Georgie liked her. But, she didn't like him, not like that.

One day when Brenda was visiting and Kate was inside having coffee and cake with Mrs. Cambridge, Georgie came walking down the block with a girl Brenda had never seen before. Brenda was sitting on the bottom step leaning over a tiny house she made out of sticks and rocks and dirt, when Georgie walked by and purposely knocked it over with his foot.

Brenda jumped up and punched him square on the jaw like a professional boxer, "What's wrong with you, boy?! Keep messin' with me and I'm gonna put a hurting on you like you wouldn't believe!" The girl raised her eyebrow and smirked. Georgie was dumbstruck that she had gotten so mad, but he was also secretly impressed that she could hit so hard. Strangely, his heart fluttered a bit. As he held the side of his face with his hand the girl smiled, held out her hand and introduced herself, "Hi, I'm Gloria. This here fool's my cousin. We just moved here from Connecticut." Brenda forgot Georgie was even standing there. She loosened her shoulders, un-balled her fists, blushed an 80-watt grin and shook Gloria's hand, "I... I'm Brenda." Gloria smiled, pumped Brenda's hand twice then let it fall. Gloria was light-skinned with long black hair and beautiful white, straight teeth. She stared at Brenda. Working his jaw from left to right, Georgie looked from Brenda to Gloria, Gloria to Brenda, paused, sucked his teeth, and then bent down to try fixing the stick-rock-dirt house. Gloria went into an awkward, full explanation about how she had just gotten her braces off after 3 years and she was glad people had stopped calling her 'train tracks' and 'metal mouth.' Brenda chuckled, then apologized (coming to her defense against the 'no-gooders'). Gloria smiled "They're eatin' those words now, right?" Brenda smiled, heart racing, and responded "Damn, right."

Summer Camp

In 1951, when Brenda was 9 years old, Kate reluctantly arranged for her to spend two weeks at a sleep-away camp called Forest Lake, a Fresh Air Fund camp in upstate New York. The Fresh Air Fund coordinated sleep away camp trips in the summer for underprivileged kids who wouldn't ordinarily get out of the city. It was the first time Brenda would be away from her parents since she first came to them, and she was terrified. Kate took her to Sears to buy shorts, long pants, t-shirts, sandals, sneakers, socks, underwear, ribbons and pins for her hair, comic books, pillow, sheets and a blanket, an assortment of snacks and candy, plenty of pretty pink stationery and colored pencils for writing to family and friends back in Brooklyn. Kate packed Brenda's small trunk, boarded her on a bus with strangers, and waved goodbye.

Brenda wanted to cry on the bus, but she wouldn't dare let the other kids see her cry. She tried to smile and seem happy to be going away from home for a while, but she kept to herself and followed the crowd.

The bus counselor, Luann welcomed the girls, some new and most from the previous year, and asked everyone to join her in singing songs to break the ice. Brenda followed along, but sang low since she didn't know the words.

When the buses arrived at the camp site parking lot, everyone was instructed to take their bags and belongings off of the bus and go stand by the counselors who would be holding up a large sign with a number that would correspond with the cottage number they were assigned. Brenda noticed she was the only girl with a large trunk. All the other girls had small suitcases. She knew immediately that Kate had over-packed, and she felt very embarrassed. Brenda was assigned to cottage #4 with nine other girls her age. As she stood back from the group she surveyed the area. It was actually a pretty and peaceful place. There were massive, tall trees with all different shades of green leaves, and all kinds of plants and flowers everywhere. She thought to herself, 'Dad would love this place.' The lawns leading to the larger cottages were manicured and men in gray jumpsuits, gray caps and black work gloves were scattered about caring for the grounds. The biggest, white-painted wooden building was very tall and long and had two entrances. Brenda learned this was the meal hall where all the campers met and ate together three times a day for breakfast, lunch and dinner. Off to the right was another slightly smaller building that was the performance hall where the end of summer camp show was held each year. The huge lake was at the bottom of the hill, and there were lines in the water with orange buoys approximately 8 inches apart to separate the shallow end from the deeper end of the lake. Cottage counselor Heidi offered to help with her trunk since it was too heavy for her to carry across the campus on her own, while head counselor Arden led the group in song. Once at cottage #4, the girls were given a list of cottage rules, and instructions. When Heidi blew the whistle, all the girls raced up the four steps and into the cottage to secure their bed and bunk areas. Brenda got a spot next to the dusty window, and was happy that she would be able to watch the stars overhead at night. After settling in quickly, she noticed there was no bathroom in the cottage. The map of the grounds attached to the instructions showed the bathroom was outside and over the road. It was a small building with ten bathroom stalls and a row of sinks for washing up (no showers). Every morning at Forest Lake a bugle sounded at 6am. All the campers were instructed to stand around the flagpole and salute the flag. They would say the Pledge of Allegiance, and then the Forest Lake camp song. "We weeelcome youuuu to Foooorest Lake, we're miiiighty glaaaad you're heeeeere.... We'll stand and give a miiighty cheer. We'll ring you IN, we'll wring you OUT. Then we'll give you all

a MIGHTY SHOUT! Haiiil, Haiiil the gang's all here, we welcome you

to FOREST LAAAAAKE!"

Then all the campers would walk together down to the dining hall for

breakfast. Breakfast consisted of cold cereal, oatmeal, powdered eggs, a

choice of sausage or bacon, orange juice, fruit, and milk. On the way out

of the dining hall there were baskets where each person could select one

piece of fruit (orange, apple, or banana). They would get free play

outside for about 30 minutes before the scheduled recreational activities

would begin the long day. The schedule consisted of arts and crafts,

dance, nature discovery walks, swimming, theatre, shop class, and

cooking class. Brenda signed up for swimming, arts and crafts, shop and

cooking class. She figured she never got to cook at home, so this might

be fun. They actually didn't get to cook any hot food. They made all

kinds of sandwiches, and ooey gooey snacks, but the real meals were

made by the teacher, Ms. Neville. She thought they would burn or cut

themselves, so she only let them use plastic knives and forks and she was

the only one who got to touch the oven. Brenda was much better in shop

class where Mr. Schmidt let her bang out a metal plaque with her name for her bedroom door at home. She got to heat it up and paint it too.

Dave even gave it his stamp of approval when she brought it home.

One afternoon when all the girls came back from the lake to wash up

and change before dinner, Brenda was lying on her bunk admiring a tiny

snow globe from her trunk that Kate had given her from her trinket

collection. Brenda always loved it, but Kate would never let her touch

the glass case that held all of her crystal figurines and trinkets she

collected over the years. Before leaving for camp she had been so sad

that Kate told her she could take it with her as a 'piece of home' to have

while she was gone. Brenda cherished it and loved to shake it over and

over to watch the tiny plastic snowflakes float through the water and land

at the bottom where the snowman stood. A girl named Theresa

(everyone called her Tabby) who was the same age as Brenda but tall

and lanky for her age, had been eyeing all of Brenda's things ever since

she arrived at camp. Tabby had been going to Forest Lake for three years,

longer than most of the girls. So, she felt she had seniority over the

others. She was obviously the ringleader, and the other girls did

whatever she said. Brenda had been warned by Kate to stay out of

trouble and don't fight anyone, so Brenda stayed clear of Tabby.

As Brenda played with the globe, she heard Tabby and two of her

flunkies giggling and pointing at her. She rolled her eyes and kept shaking up the globe, trying to ignore them. Tabby, who had not said a word to her for the first four days of camp, came over and said "Hi, how ya doin'?" She wasn't really talking to Brenda. She was already bending down next to her trunk starting to finger through her belongings. Brenda swung her legs over to the side of the bunk where her trunk sat and tried to slam it shut, but Tabby was too fast and lifted it back up. She stared Brenda down and said "Well, THAT was pretty rude. You should want to share your nice things with your new friends." Brenda was silent, but kept her eyes on Tabby, and the other girls who looked as if they were waiting for the signal to get involved. Brenda said "That's my stuff, and I don't even know you to be sharing my things with you." "Oh, you think you too good to share stuff with us, rich girl?" Tabby said as she quickly reached down on the bed behind Brenda's back and grabbed the snow globe. "Why don't you give me this?" She shook the globe and laughed, then Brenda went to grab it from her hand. The snow globe slipped from Tabby's hand and shattered onto the wooden floor, water and snow disappearing quickly through the dirty wooden planks. Only the tiny snowman survived, lying on his side. "LOOK WHAT YOU DID!" Brenda was fuming and crying. "Oh, so what! I'm sure your parents can buy you another one." And with that Tabby walked back over to the other girls and finished dressing for dinner. They laughed all the way to dinner, and on the way back to the cottage. Brenda was not afraid of Tabby. But, she was afraid of what Kate was going to do to her for breaking the snow globe. If she got into a fight too, Kate would beat her for sure.

That night, Brenda was so upset and nervous she wet the bed. She woke up around 3am, quietly balled the sheet up and shoved it down into the bottom of her trunk and replaced it with a fresh sheet on her bunk. She changed into fresh, dry clothes and put the soiled clothes at the bottom of the trunk before anyone could wake up. The next night she wet the bed again. Mortified because she only had two sets of sheets, she snuck out to the bathroom while everyone was asleep and washed one of the sheets. She tried to air dry them as best she could, but there was not enough time. All the campers and counselors would be getting up in an hour. She put the damp sheet back on her bed and laid down on it until everyone woke up. She got dressed with everyone else, went out for the pledge and morning song and then made her way back to the cottage. When she got there Tabby and two of her friends had pulled out Brenda's soiled sheet and clothes from the bottom of her trunk and were dancing around them in a circle singing "Pissy baby, pissy baby, Brenda is a pissy baby." Some of the other girls in the cottage were giggling too, but a few just stared in silence. Tabby had been picking on a few of the other girls in the cottage along with Brenda, to which they didn't take kindly. Brenda grabbed her things from the floor and was about to run out of the cottage when Heidi walked in. "What's going on in here?" Tabby and her girls quickly sat down on their beds and folded their hands and said nothing. The other girls just looked down. Brenda was crying and holding the soiled clothes to her chest. Heidi took her outside and asked her what happened. When Brenda explained, Heidi said, "You should have just come to me the first night and we could have taken care of it." Heidi was a very tall, slim girl who wore her dark blond hair pulled back into a long, fat braid that ended at her thighs. Her eyes were the color of violets. She was a college student on summer break receiving credit towards her major, social work. She was Brenda's favorite counselor. She called a cottage meeting and made all the girls sit around with her in a circle. She spoke to the girls about not teasing one another, being kind, considerate and respectful. The whole time Tabby and the other bullies were glaring at her and rolling their eyes in anger and disgust. Brenda was mortified and kept looking down at her shoes for the rest of the meeting.

The next day Brenda told Heidi she wanted to go home. She asked if she could call Kate. Heidi said she understood and she arranged for Brenda to walk down the road with her to the general store to use the pay phone. There was only one telephone on premises at Forest Lake, and it was to only be used by the camp administrator, or in an extreme emergency (like someone requiring medical care). When Kate answered the telephone Brenda was a blubbering mess. She cried and told her how she had wet the bed and the girls called her pissy baby, and she wanted her to drive upstate to get her. Kate told her how sorry she was that she was having a hard time. Then she told her she was going to come and get her. She went back to the cottage and started packing up her things and waited for Kate to come. After two days she realized Kate was not coming. She eventually got it, she was being forced to work it out for herself. She was tough, and Kate knew it. And she knew there would be no second trip to the pay phone to discuss it. She pulled herself together, unpacked her things, and immersed herself in camp activities. Some of the other nice girls must have felt sorry for her, and invited her to sit with them at mealtime and picked her for outdoor games. When they realized how athletic Brenda was, she was in great demand. It was the boost of confidence she needed to get past the 'pissy' incident, and she ignored Tabby for the reminder of her time at Forest Lake.

When she got off the bus at the end of the two weeks, Kate didn't recognize her. Her skin was completely black from being in the sun for two weeks, and her brown hair was a dusty red color and a complete mess from swimming every day. She was so happy and excited to see Kate. She struggled to drag her trunk over to where Kate was waiting, held her arms out and yelled "Ma!!" Kate's face was twisted and surprised. She said, "What in the world happened to you. You look a mess!" Brenda didn't care at all. Kate grabbed her trunk and shoved it in the trunk of the car. Brenda climbed in the backseat, a bit disappointed at her reception, but so glad to be going home.

Uncle Jerry

In June of 1956, when Brenda was 14 years old, she and Kate went to visit Kate's sister Joan and her family at their summer home in Atlantic City. Brenda loved to visit Aunt Joanie and Uncle George both at their winter home in Norristown, PA, and at their summer home in Atlantic City. For Brenda, summers in AC were glorious. It was a great escape from the city, and felt far away from her normal. As soon as Kate's car passed Baltic and turned onto Atlantic Avenue, Brenda could smell the ocean and taste the salty air on her tongue. She looked forward to six weeks of sand between her toes, Aunt Joanie's home cooking, and seeing the sights on the famous Boardwalk.

The Boardwalk offered all sorts of spectacles and items to see, buy, and win. Nights on the boardwalk were especially electric. Women wore fancy hats, dresses and shoes for the evening stroll. The gentlemen wore fine suits and carried walking sticks. Not everyone dressed this way, only the ritzy crowd, which for Brenda, was part of the entertainment. There were rides and games to win prizes, even oddities in clear boxes and cages. Her favorite attraction was always Mr. Peanut, the Planter's

Peanut man. Mr. Peanut could be found standing outside of the famous Planter's Peanut Shop. He was a man dressed in long black pants, long-sleeved black shirt, and black dress shoes covered with white tuxedo spats. On top of this outfit was a huge beige plastic peanut shell cut in half below the waist. His head was covered with a black top hat with the words 'Mr. Peanut' scrolled all the way around the hat at the band. A big black monocle covered his right eye and was painted down the right side of his peanut body. He stood at least 8 feet tall and was an amazing sight for any child. Peanut roasters sat in the front windows of the store to carry the aroma of freshly roasted peanuts down either end of the boardwalk and for blocks over as people approached the boardwalk.

When Kate went to Fralinger's, the saltwater taffy store on the boardwalk at Tennessee Avenue, she would take Brenda along with her. The store was painted in pastel colors outside and inside. Pastel blue, green, yellow, orange, and lavender colored boxes lined the walls. The sweet-smelling, sticky taffy was mixed, stretched, folded, and boxed right there in the store. Kate would buy all different colors and flavors for her friends and family back in New York. And, of course, she would bring some home for Dave and Brenda. It was a family tradition.

Aunt Joanie's daughter Betty was three years Brenda's senior, very stylish for a country girl, and sweet as could be toward Brenda. She and Brenda would play records on the record player in her room, doing the latest dances and singing songs all day. Sometimes Betty wore designer dresses with bold stripes, and sometimes she would put on nautical capri pants in navy, red, white or yellow. She fancied button down summer cardigans, and always tucked a flower in the side of her hair like the great Billie Holiday. The dark, smoky, tortured tale of a woman hopelessly in love, 'Lady Sings the Blues' was released that year, and Betty played it over and over, until she fell asleep. Brenda overheard Kate ask Aunt Joanie, "Why in the world is Betty so obsessed with that depressing song???" Joanie pursed her lips tight as she poured a hot cup of tea, and spoke in her soft, mild-mannered voice, "She likes what she likes."

By the end of August, Betty had ditched the flower in her hair and returned to her previous musical obsession, Frankie Lymon and the Teenagers. The Teenagers had just released a new single, 'I Want You To Be My Girl', and Brenda was over the moon because she could never get enough of Frankie Lymon. He was cute, and could sing like nobody's business. Betty and Brenda loved belting out the long notes with him, 'Ohh-Ohhhhhh, Oh-Oh, Oh-Oh Ohhhh'. Brenda was shy about singing and really only felt comfortable doing so with Betty, or at church, or when she was alone at home. Secretly, for the first time, she considered what it would be like to sing professionally.

Brenda had a huge crush on her cousin Billy. He was 22 years old and the most eligible bachelor in Baltimore. He was very handsome, had a great paying job, a beautiful penthouse apartment, was never married and had no children. He drove all kinds of fast, flashy sports cars, dressed to the nines, always smelled fresh and clean like he just got out of the shower and splashed on strong, manly cologne, and wore his light-brown hair slicked back. He wore casual straight-legged slacks with rugged striped short-sleeve shirts with bold stripes and dress shoes. He dressed as slick and as cool as Jackie Wilson or Sam Cooke or Smokey Robinson.

He did not discriminate and dated all kinds of women, including Black, Asian, and Hispanic. He even dated white women when it was pretty dangerous to do so. Women loved him, and men wanted to learn his secrets. He walked with an air of confidence that Brenda had never seen before. She loved to watch him walk, talk to people, and study his movements. He knew a little bit about everything, relationships, politics, entertainment, sports, travel, fine food, wine, and manufacturing industries. He could hold a room captive for long periods including Brenda, who had on one occasion, fell asleep at the top of the stairs after eavesdropping for three hours. Billy was definitely a bright spot in her Atlantic City visits. She hated that he would only stay for one or two nights, and then he would have to drive back to Baltimore. Billy knew Brenda had a little bit of a crush on him, but he never made her feel weird or odd about it. He was gracious and classy and she loved him more for it. He gave her hugs, and love, and made her feel more like a baby sister than a cousin.

Brenda's sweet, fond memories of childhood summers in Atlantic City would end by the end of the summer of 1956. One day a man Brenda had never seen before visited the Davis house. Brenda didn't know exactly who brought him there or why he was visiting, but she didn't like him immediately when he was introduced to her. He was a very tall man, well over 6 and a half feet. He had smooth dark chocolate skin, slim build, and was dressed in a brown and white bowling shirt with brown slacks. His black shoes were extra shiny, and you could see your reflection on the top. When he smiled you could see three gold-capped teeth on the right side of his mouth, although the rest of his teeth were so yellow you couldn't tell where his yellow teeth ended and the gold caps began, except for the dull shine of the metal.

Uncle George introduced him, and Brenda was instructed to call him Uncle Jerry. She knew he wasn't really her uncle, but grown-ups had always told her to call adults "uncle" and "aunt" even if they weren't related. It was a sign of respect.

Uncle Jerry stayed for three nights, and Brenda avoided him as best she could the first two days. On the third day, all the adults were supposed to drive over to the beach in two cars. Brenda and Betty stayed behind, with Brenda listening to songs on the radio on the second-floor porch, and Betty reading a book on the main floor. Brenda was so preoccupied with the harmonies of 'Oh What A Night' by The Dells that she hadn't noticed Uncle Jerry had walked back to the house alone.

Uncle Jerry opened the wooden patio screen door, walked out onto the porch slowly, and let it slam shut to get Brenda's attention. She jumped up and saw Jerry standing over her wearing only sunglasses and white swim trunks with a blue stripe down either side. His chest was bare, and she especially noticed how muscular his chest and arms were. He started swaying slowly to the music, singing along, and rotating his hips as if he was slow grinding with a woman.

Brenda excused herself, grabbed her radio, and headed to the safety of her room where she planned to lock the door and wait for Kate to return. When she entered her room, she closed the door and noticed there was no lock. The latch was broken, and she remembered it was on the list of things she heard Uncle George say he needed to get around to fixing before the end of the summer. Before Brenda could barricade the door, Uncle Jerry was inside the room and throwing her down onto the queen size bed. She struggled under his weight to get free, but his strong arms had pinned her down tight as her body sunk into the middle of the too soft mattress. She selected this room out of the other eight guest bedrooms in the three-story house because it was the plushest guest bed, and made her feel safe and warm while she slept, like a baby bird in a nest. Unfortunately, it was also one of the only beds that did not have noisy springs and did not creek the floor. So, Betty couldn't hear a thing going on above her head as she quietly enjoyed her book on the floor below.

Uncle Jerry put his hand over Brenda's mouth, tore away her clothes, and entered her hard and rough. Her screams could not penetrate his large, rough black hand. His sweaty skin and hot breath was in her face, and all she could see was those shiny yellow caps. She tried to bite his fingers but he was smashing her face down so she couldn't get her teeth loose from her lips that covered them. Uncle Jerry kept grinding and grinding into her pelvic bones for what seemed like an hour. Brenda could feel the blood dripping down her crotch and onto her favorite quilted bedspread. He buried his face into the bedspread above Brenda's head and let out a muffled groan as he came inside of her. He took his time climbing off her and out of the bed. As she lay there in pain and terrified, covered in his sweat and her blood, he pulled up his swim trunks, put his finger up to his mouth and said "Shhhhh." Then, he slowly walked out of the room and closed the door.

Brenda lay there crying for what seemed like hours. She didn't know whether to scream or run or call the police. Should she run and find Kate? Should she go downstairs and tell Betty? Was he still outside the door? Would he come back and do it again? Maybe Betty could call the police, or find Kate. She wanted to move, say something, or do something. Instead, she lay there confused, scared, in pain, bloody, and immediately ashamed. When she thought she could walk, she got up and peeked out into the hallway to see if Uncle Jerry was around. The house was unnervingly silent. She wondered if Uncle Jerry had made his way downstairs and was doing the same thing to Betty. She went into the bathroom and locked the door. She showered to wash off the dried blood and semen several times, because it seemed she could not get the smell off of her. She looked in the mirror and noticed her pelvic bones were red and bruised. She got dressed and snuck down to the first floor. She peeked into the den and saw Betty still reading her book. She walked into the room and asked Betty if she had seen Uncle Jerry. Betty said he said goodbye about thirty minutes prior, saying he had to get back on the road to North Carolina. Brenda started to tell Betty what happened, but she decided not to. She wasn't sure how Kate would react, and whether anyone would even believe her. Uncle Jerry had seemed so nice to everyone, and Uncle George liked him, too. The next day she noticed that her shoulders were black and blue. Even though it was nearly 98 degrees every day, for the remainder of the summer Brenda stayed covered up to hide the bruises, and the shame. She never told anyone about the incident, and no one seemed to notice.

Visit to the Hills

On Brenda's 15th birthday, she asked Kate if she could go visit the Hills. She was older now, and she desperately wanted to confront her mother and father. Not with words, or disrespect. But, she wanted to make them 'see' her. She thought maybe they would 'SEE' her more clearly if they could witness for themselves how well she had grown up. That she was a kind, generous, thoughtful person with friends and goals and dreams. After the incident in Atlantic City, she felt herself change inside. A bit of her died on that springy, painful, bloody bed, and she wanted someone to acknowledge her... maybe give something back that she had lost.

She asked for two weeks. She didn't know if Kate would allow it, since she never let her stay overnight at anyone's home without her being present. But, Kate actually thought it was a good idea. She thought Dill just might give Brenda a chance. It had been so long, fifteen years already. Kate had known Dill all her life, and she believed there was good in him. He had gone astray, become angry and drank too much. But, she still wanted to believe he would do the right thing by Brenda. Brenda didn't know what to expect. But, she knew she wanted to go.

And she knew for certain she never wanted to spend another summer in Atlantic City.

These visits were desired but became very confusing for Brenda. There was never any explanation given about why she had two mothers, and why she needed to call them both 'mom'. Kate only told Brenda as much as she felt she needed to know. At the same time, she did her best to protect the integrity of her brother and sister-in-law.

Brenda called Alice 'mom', although she didn't feel comfortable doing so. She would just say hello or keep the conversation general. Alice was always nice to Brenda, but in a cordial way, like a guest. She certainly had a better and closer relationship with her other children, Norman and Marilyn. Alice had since given birth to another baby girl, Dana, who was now five. She was a tiny, light-skinned child with hazel eyes, with perfectly blended features of both her mother and her father. Brenda was treated more like a niece, or a child Alice was babysitting for a few weeks while her parents were away on a business trip. It was tense, and strained, and difficult, but Brenda was determined to stand her ground, and be acknowledged. She had to see the two weeks through.

Marilyn had always treated Brenda like a sister since they were kids. She welcomed her into her room to play with toys, or took her outside to play with her friends. Marilyn loved introducing Brenda as her sister, as if it were the most natural thing in the world. When her friends would ask why Brenda didn't live with her, she would reply, "I don't know. She just doesn't." And that would be the end of it. They played kick the can and hide and seek. They would walk to the corner store together and share stories about their schools and dances they had attended. They would listen to their favorite songs like 'Only You' and 'My Prayer' by The Platters, 'Why You Do Me Like You Do by The Cleftones, and anything and everything by Brenda's favorite group The Teenagers. Time spent with Marilyn was the highlight at the Hill house. But, no matter how much of a great time she would be having, Dill always ruined the fun by ordering the girls to come inside early, or yelling at them to quiet down if they were upstairs giggling over pictures in magazines or comic books.

In addition to making Brenda feel unwelcome and uncomfortable, Dill told the other children, "Brenda has a disease" and warned that they should "stay away from her." And, if they didn't heed the warning, they could catch the disease and die. Marilyn knew this was wrong and never listened to her father's cruel words toward Brenda. She loved her sister and treated her with respect and kindness. She really didn't care why her sister was living with her aunt, and never questioned it. But, Norman

was a Daddy's boy, always looking for ways to impress his father. He

didn't like Brenda or trust her, but was never sure why. He just knew

his Dad became sad, angry, tense and 'different' when she was around.

And, of course, he drank more when she was around too. She hadn't

done anything bad to him, and he'd never seen her do anything bad to

anyone else, especially his Dad. Norman was cordial toward her, as he

would be with any acquaintance, but never warm. He would ignore her,

as if she hadn't just said something to him or contributed to a group

conversation they were both part of. It was a rebuff more than it was

mean. She loved calling him her big brother, and telling other people

she had a big brother, but he never acknowledged her as his sister, and

this hurt Brenda very deeply. Ever the optimist, Brenda looked up to her

big brother. She would take pictures of him to her friends back home

and brag about how smart and handsome her big brother was, and how

he was going to be a military man just like her Daddy. In a way, this was

sort of true since both Dill and Dave had both served in the Army.

For Brenda, the hardest part of the visits to the Hill house was that

Alice, her real mom, seemed indifferent when Brenda came around.

Alice treated her as if she was someone else's child. Brenda wondered

if she thought of her every day the way she thought of Alice, wondering if she missed kissing her and saying 'goodnight' at bedtime. She wondered if she missed sharing in all of her life's special 'first' moments, like her first tooth, and the first time she walked, and her first day of school, and her first scrape on the knee. Brenda wondered what her life would have been like if Alice had kept her like she did Norman and Marilyn.

When the summer visit was over and Brenda went back home to the Robinsons, the return was bittersweet. She had spent a lot of time around Alice. It meant the world to Brenda just to see her, be near her, breathe in her scent, and have her do motherly things for her, like set the table, cook, make her bed, and set house rules. When she returned home, she missed her sister Marilyn and Alice, but was always glad to be rid of Dill and Norman.

At the Hills, she had to share a room with Marilyn, but back at home she had her own room. It was where things were normal and pleasant. There was no hostility directed toward her. Nobody looked at her with resentment or treated her badly. She could just relax and feel loved, wanted, and normal. She told Kate, despite her feelings for Alice and Marilyn, she never wanted to stay at the Hills again. It was torturous to watch Brenda return feeling defeated and dejected. So, Kate obliged and never made her stay over at the Hill house again.

Finding the Music

In 1958, the Robinsons moved to a quiet, friendly neighborhood in Springfield Gardens, Queens. Their quaint, red brick, one-family new home was lovely. It had a large yard to run around and a huge, shady maple tree that cozied what seemed like thousands of cicada bugs at night. They would buzz their signature crescendo, up, up, up, then stop... and start all over. It took a bit of getting used to, but Brenda quickly adapted to the quietness of the neighborhood.

At her new school, Brenda met and became best friends with two girls, Joanne Evans and Donna White. Joanne was a slim, fair-skinned, attractive girl with pouty lips, straight nose, and a hint of a raspy, slow-talking Southern drawl. She wore her hair in a short press and curl, and her mother, Grace, attended church with Kate. Donna was a brown-skinned, lovely girl with a round face, full lips, and big, beautiful eyes. She wore her hair with a part down the middle with loose pressed curls just above her shoulders or brushed back and tapered behind her ears. She had lots of style. Brenda considered Donna her best friend.

When the girls realized they all lived within one block of one another, it was even sweeter for Brenda. She now had best girlfriends, sisters, to share her inner-most secrets and dreams. They would walk to school together, talk about the Hit Parade, who was appearing on Ed Sullivan, and the traveling doo wop shows from Philadelphia that were coming to town. They read Archie comic books, and all wanted to fight Veronica for trying to steal Betty's boyfriend Archie. There were no black kids in the Archie comic books back then, so they would pencil in Archie's face and pretend his name was 'Jimmy'. Jimmy was a very popular name for a cool boy. All the hottest musicians and actors were either named Jimmy by their mama, or just called themselves Jimmy. And all the girls wanted to have their very own.

The girls went to the movie theatre, skate parties, bowling, and church dances together. They were inseparable. Although they all talked about boys they liked, Brenda noticed that Joanne and Donna liked certain boys and dreamed of being their wives. It was all very romantic. But, Brenda never really thought about boys in that same way. She thought boys were ok, but she didn't dream of marrying them or having their children. She had always been a bit of a tomboy, and didn't mind getting messy. Although she wore the skirts, dresses, kitten heels, hats, pearls, pocketbooks, and all the frilly clothes Kate bought for her, she only liked wearing them to church or special occasions. It made her feel rich and fancy. But, day to day, she felt most comfortable in capris with satin button down tops and flat shoes or sneakers. She wasn't interested in kissing or going out on a date with a boy. Boys were incidental, just friends.

Brenda had always known she was different, ever since she was a little girl. But, she knew she could not share her feelings with anyone, because in her neighborhood people who were different were not treated nicely. White boys and street gangs like the Chans, who hung out not far from her home, were notorious for 'jumping' and beating up kids who admitted they were gay. The gay boys ended up in the hospital, and the gay girls were cast out. So, Brenda learned that being different was something she needed to keep to herself. She knew her best friends loved her, and thought they would try to understand. But, she knew it would change things, and she didn't want things to change. She worried they might start being weird with her, like hiding from her when they had to change clothes at gym, or hesitate talking about boys with her. She wanted to be treated normal, just like she treated them. So, she hid her true feelings and pretended to feel what the other girls felt when it came to boys and sex. The only person she could tell her true feelings was her sister Marilyn.

Marilyn had come out years earlier, and she was Brenda's 'she-ro' for that. Marilyn didn't care what anyone thought of her. She was sure of herself, and had made up her mind to live life on her own terms, no matter what anyone thought, especially Dill. She wore three-piece men's suits, men's shoes, slacks and jackets, whatever she chose. She went anyplace she chose, and went on dates with girls. When she got to see Brenda, she would tell her all about her dates, and Brenda would listen wide eyed, and awestruck at her sister's brazenness. Marilyn tried to be a source of encouragement for Brenda. "If there's ANYTHING you want to talk about, or share, or ask advice on, just let me know. I'm here for you, always." But, she understood very well that Brenda would have to find the courage to come out on her own and in her own time.

One cool fall evening, Brenda, Donna and Joanne attended a skate party. As they enjoyed the music, Brenda noticed a short, lean, brown-skinned young man with slick black hair and a handsome face walk through the door. She had seen him around before, but he was usually dressed up like he was on his way to church. Today, he looked like a cool-boy. Although she wasn't looking for a boyfriend, there was something incredibly attractive about this guy. He walked around to the other side of the rink and said hello to some guys and girls. Trying to ignore him, Brenda kept dancing with her friends, laughing and having a good time. Although pretending not to see him, she couldn't get over the effect he was having on her. Halfway through the party, the young man walked over and asked her to dance. She tried to play it cool, "sure." Her friends feigned shock as she turned to dance with him. He leaned in so she could hear him over the voices of Frankie Lymon & The Teenagers' *Why Do Fools Fall In Love*, and asked, "What's your name?" "Brenda," she replied. "What's yours?" He said, "They call me Jimmy."

> *Dr. Juwayriah: I see you smiling. Tell me more about Jimmy.*
> *Brenda: He was truly fine. I just couldn't believe he chose me out of all the girls there.... Jimmy and I had a lot in common. Certainly, we both had some pretty interesting characters in our families. But, mainly we had the music.*

Duke & Carolena

Roy 'Duke' Taylor was born in Al Sais Loraine, France. His family moved to Harlem USA when he was just 8. As an only child and having a penchant for music and instruments, he taught himself to play drums and was always plucking at any strings to make music. When he turned 16, he left home to chase his dream of starting his own band.

His son, James "Jimmy" Taylor was born on February 5, 1940, to Duke and Carolena Scott. He was their second child, their first son Roy Jr. being born two years earlier.

Duke and Carolena met at a nightclub on 135th Street and 5th Avenue in Harlem called The Sugar Cane Club in 1938; she was 18 and he was 25. Duke played drums with a very popular jazz band called The Wesley Goode Trio, alongside other acts, those of which happened to be lucky enough to get a spot on the stage on any given night. The Sugar Cane was always packed with lots of black patrons as well as some white ones. Carolena and her twin sister Catalina had front row seats one night when the club was really jumping. She fell for Duke the first night she laid eyes on him.

The twins were two of eight siblings, five girls and three boys. They had moved to NYC after spending their whole lives in Lancaster, VA. Everyone knew everyone, but there was nothing exciting going on there. And they wanted more, especially Carolena.

Duke, a very handsome and distinguished looking man, stood six feet tall, his tailored suit complimented his muscular frame. He had a very commanding presence. As she watched him beat on the drums like a wild man, slick hair flying around, Carolena couldn't get enough. She knew from the moment she first laid eyes on Duke, she had to meet the drummer.

After the show, Duke came right over to Carolena's table and introduced himself. He paid for their dinner and drinks, and spent the next hour charming her sister in an effort to get closer to Carolena. He drove them home in his mint condition, hunter green 1935 Mercury Egypt, dropping off Catalina first. Once alone, the two talked for hours until the sun came up. He continued to visit her over the next six months when the band was in town.

At first, Duke was very sweet and kind to Carolena. He bought her flowers and dancing ballerina music boxes, and showed her off around town. She was proud to be on his arm, and had fallen more in love with

Duke over the first three years they were together. After their sons were born, things changed for the worst. Duke went back on the road with the band, frequently leaving Carolena and the babies behind. She became one of his several women living in Harlem and other states too. Ironically, however, although Duke was doing the cheating, he would often accuse Carolena of stepping out on him while he was away.

In his absence Carolena would have friends over. After the boys were asleep, she and her friends would sit around, talk, laugh and listen to music. Most of Carolena's friends were female, but a few were male. Carolena was a God-fearing woman, and, although they weren't legally married, she respected her relationship with Duke and was a dedicated mother to her sons.

Whenever Duke returned after a few weeks touring, he would go on a tirade, accusing Carolena of cheating and exposing his sons to a salacious life. He called her a whore and other foul and disrespectful names in front of the boys and her friends. They would fight all the time. Carolena was only 5'2" tall, weighing 115 pounds. So, physically she was no real match for Duke. However, one evening, after Duke had been out partying with friends, he returned home with perfume all over his shirt. Carolena argued with him and told him to get out. Duke slapped her hard across the face and she fell to the floor. Duke stormed out of the house and took the elevator down three flights to the 1st floor. Carolena held a cool rag with ice on her left cheek, while her right hand held a potted plant that sat near the window. When Duke walked out of the building, she threw that plant and hit him square on the right side of his head and shoulder, knocking him to the ground. She closed the window as she saw people rush over to tend to him. She turned off the lights and went to bed. Duke suffered a mild concussion and a broken collar bone, which prevented him from playing his music for several weeks. Carolena heard that he was being cared for by a woman he was seeing on the other side of Harlem, and she didn't care.

By 1945, when Jimmy was 5 years old and Roy Jr. was 7, Duke did something that would change the boys' lives forever. One evening while Carolena was asleep, Duke snuck into the boys' room and packed a bag for each of them. While still in their pajamas and wiping the sleep out of their eyes, Duke ordered them to quietly put on their shoes and coats and meet him by the front door. The boys did as they were instructed. Roy put his arm around his younger brother's shoulder and watched as his father handed him two duffel bags, one for himself and one for Jimmy. They headed out of the apartment, out of the building and got into an awaiting taxi cab. The boys dozed off in the car, and were shaken awake by Duke, "Come on boys, time to go." They arrived at an apartment building similar to the one they lived in, but it was shorter, with only three floors. "Where are we, Dad?" asked Roy Jr. "This is our new home boys. So, make yourselves comfortable," said Duke. Roy looked puzzled, but he didn't dare ask any questions. It was already 4:00 a.m., so he figured he would try to get more details in the morning. The boys slept in the same bed that first night, missing their mom and wondering what was happening. When the boys woke up, Duke sat them on the living room couch and simply said, "Boys, I'm going to tell you the truth, because I'm raising you to be men. Your mama is too loose. And she is not doing a good job taking care of you. So, from now on, I'm your mama AND your daddy." Now, go get dressed, we're going out. No other explanation was given. No opportunity for a question and answer session was allowed.

Carolena thought Duke had taken her sons to scare and threaten her. But, after two days, she realized something was very wrong. She went to the local police station to report the children missing. When she said she suspected Duke of kidnapping the boys, the police waved her off saying, "he'll likely calm down and bring his son's home." The police didn't care much about finding missing little black boys in Harlem in 1946, especially if the kids were reportedly taken by their own parent.

So, a heartbroken, Carolena did her best, with limited resources, to find her babies. She enlisted friends to help ask around and she went to every club in Harlem looking for them. Duke would always be one step ahead of her. He would move from apartment to apartment in different areas in Harlem but needed to stay close to the jazz clubs where he could find work. Although initially Duke only moved the boys to the other side of Harlem, they would not realize how close their mother had lived until fifteen years later.

Mamma-Daddy, Mamma-Daddy

Brenda: Duke was a real piece of work.
Juwayriah: He sounds like a very complicated man. Much
like Dill, you think? (tapping her notepad with her pen and
raising an eyebrow).
Brenda: Yeah… I guess so (she considered).

Raised in the South on tough love and hard lessons, Duke's father taught him not to trust anyone. He grew to become what he referred to as "anti-establishment." The boys would often hear him say, "Niggers ain't shit because they don't have their shit together. Niggers don't want to work." Years of traveling on the road, experiencing so much racism toward Black musicians, and witnessing the struggles of Black men, black relationships and Black families had a profound effect on Duke. He would tell his sons to stay away from Black American women, "…because they will not take care of you. Marry a white, foreign woman."

Duke had a strong hatred toward white men because of the prejudice he had experienced. However, he believed that Black men needed to learn all they could from the white man, and then strive to be better than them at everything. Though he had only completed his formal studies up to ninth grade, he was self-taught in music and academics. He read all kinds of books and taught himself how to play many musical instruments. He also taught himself four languages other than English. He spoke French, German, Yiddish, and Greek fluently. Because he had a knack for picking things up so quickly, he expected his sons to be able to do the same.

Duke worked part-time as a cook on the railroads, but considered himself to be a musician by trade. He was extremely talented and often traveled the country to play with various bands and celebrities, including the great Lionel Hampton, Red Garland and Count Basie. He was an accomplished instrumentalist who played drums (his primary instrument), saxophone, trumpet, piano and vibraphone.

Duke was smooth and impressed all those around him with his fine clothes and hats. His clothes were always pressed, he wore spit-shined dress shoes, a sharp overcoat, and his fingernails were always clean and buffed. He was friendly and outgoing with strangers, but strict with his rules at home and especially hard on his sons.

He was determined to make young Roy into a great drummer. He constantly made him sit all night at a drum set learning the craft. Roy practiced keeping time with various beats – *Mama-Daddy, Mama-Daddy, Mama-Daddy* in time to the rhythm, over and over. He counted so often he would count measures in his sleep. This would drive Jimmy crazy, and he would often yell, "knock off that counting and go to sleep!" Sometimes Duke's forced rehearsals were so intense, Roy would cry himself to sleep out of frustration, knowing that it would start all over the next day. Fortunately, it became so frustrating for Duke that he gave up on teaching Roy how to play the drums.

One day, Duke packed the boys' up and they traveled by train to Seattle, Washington. They moved into a small, one-family house on the edge of town near the woods. It was an area populated with indigenous people. Duke moved a woman into the home and the boys were told to call her Mama Rosalee. She was a slim, curvy, caramel-colored woman who had soft brown eyes, long, shiny black hair that spiraled down her back, and was an excellent baker. She also had a very beautiful singing voice. She was sweet to the boys, and a bit of a fighter. Jimmy and Roy liked her immediately because she spoke her mind, even to Duke.

She would be in the house baking sweet bread or cinnamon apple tarts, while Duke was outside on the porch playing the guitar for the

Indigenous children. One day there was a pretty significant earthquake that shook the community. Everyone was scared and began to panic, but Duke played the French horn to help calm all the neighbors until the quake stopped. Jimmy watched the people fawning over his father, treating him with respect and admiration. He hated that Duke had so many people thinking he was some great Dad who sacrificed so much to take care of his sons. They couldn't know that over the year they lived in Seattle, Duke would beat Mama Rosalee constantly until she couldn't take it anymore and left him. Without her to help care for the boys, he brought the boys back to Harlem.

Jimmy's earliest memory of living alone with his father and brother in their small, two-bedroom apartment on Amsterdam Avenue was of him standing on a crate in front of the stove trying to make oatmeal. Since Duke had no one to watch the boys, he would often be forced to leave them alone for days at a time while he went out to work. He would cook food and put it up in the attic so it could 'keep' while he was away, and instructed them not to leave the house or open the door for anyone while he was gone.

He was a firm believer that beatings would prevent the boys from misbehaving, even if they occurred in advance of the boys actually behaving badly. Before he would go off for work, he would tell the boys to strip down naked and lie on their beds. He would whip them repeatedly with a wide leather Navy belt, explaining afterward that he had beaten them just in case they were bad while he was away. This process would scar and confuse his sons, creating a hatred and resentment within Jimmy that would fester and last for many years.

Duke had several 'wives' during the time when he was solely raising his boys. Duke would move them in one day and tell the boys "This is your new mama. You can call her Mama (insert name here – Mama Maxine or Mama June or Ma Dee)." The boys would work around the new mothers, be polite, and even tried to develop loving relationships. But, before they could get comfortable Duke would move the mothers out. One woman in particular stayed around longer than the others, and had an impact on the boys was Mama Maxine. She told them to call her Max, but Duke insisted that it would be disrespectful for the boys to call an adult by her first name, so they settled on 'Mama Max'. She was especially kind and loving toward the boys, and enjoyed the time she got to spend with them on the few occasions Duke was away and they were alone. They liked Mama Max, as much as young boys who missed their own mother could. She cooked great meals, and hemmed their pants, and gave them special coins she collected. She listened to their crazy stories and laughed at their silly jokes (when Duke was not around, of course). Mama Max lasted for nearly a year before she was gone. One day the boys awoke, and Max had simply moved out. All her things were gone, and there was no explanation about where she had gone or whether she would return.

Some evenings, Duke and the boys would walk home and Duke would stop in front of one of the many Harlem nightclubs where he played, often to talk with friends. The boys knew instinctively to stop and stand quietly while they waited for their father to finish his conversation. Sometimes this took up to six hours, or more. For two fidgety little boys, this was extremely difficult. They were not allowed to talk to people passing by on the street, or quietly amongst themselves. Although they would get tired and their legs would be exhausted, they were strictly forbidden to slouch or lean on anything. They had to keep their hands at their sides or clasped behind their back, never in their pockets, even if it was bitter cold outside.

People would remark often that Duke had the most well-mannered and best dressed sons around. They always dressed in dress shirts, ties, hard shoes, coats and hats - never sneakers or jeans. Duke said that was for "poor lookin' niggers," and he refused to allow his sons to be viewed in that way. He corrected their English and taught them diction. He often reminded them that appearance, manners, and obedience would take a man far in the world.

Stone Center

Almost a year later, Duke had become restless for the road, and had run out of patience and resources to care for the boys. One cold winter evening, he woke the boys and instructed them to put on their pants, shirts, boots and black pea coats. He put a duffel bag in each of their hands and told them to follow him. The boys did as they were instructed and didn't say a word. They walked over to Fifth Avenue between 104th and 105th Street, and stopped in front of a huge, red brick building that had bars on all the windows.

The John W. Stone Center for Orphans was wedged between what used to be Flower Fifth Hospital and the Museum of Natural History. It was the largest building on the block and to enter into it, you had to pass through two tall steel doors that had iron rivets around the edges and heavy round iron handles in the center of each door that are usually found on the doors of old castles. Duke tied nametags around the buttons of the boys' black pea coats, told them not to move, rang the bell, and then walked away. When the door opened, a very large man with one glass eye and a German accent told them to come inside and sit in the waiting area until he called for them. They looked at one another, then back at the glass-eyed man, then apprehensively they walked through the huge doors and sat where the man had instructed. They did not speak. The man explained his name was "Lynch", and he was head counselor at the Stone Center. Everybody called him 'Pop'. After about an hour or so, Pop came out of the office and told the boys to follow him down the long hallway and a flight of stairs to a room called "Intake".

Intake was a large room filled with three rows of army cots. Each cot had a small pillow, a white sheet, thin green blanket, and a locker assigned to it. Jimmy and Roy were each given a number, assigned to the only two available cots at different sides of the room, and told to settle in quickly and prepare for bed. Intake looked very much like army barracks and wasn't a pleasant place. The boys would sleep there for the first few days until permanent beds were acquired for them. The next morning, the boys awoke to the booming voice of a counselor yelling, "Rise and Fly". All the boys woke up quickly, made their beds and stood at the foot of each bed for inspection. Jimmy and Roy scrambled, following suit as best they could and took their places next to their cots. The counselor went around and did the 'bounce' test on a few of the cots with a quarter. If it didn't bounce right back up, that meant the bed was made improperly and the child would not pass inspection. Usually boys were given three days to learn to properly make a bed, but Jimmy and Roy had been fixing their beds military style every day of their lives and needed no instruction.

After they were placed in their respective dorms, they would be expected to know the rules and regulations and follow them like everyone else. They were placed on separate floors, which was difficult for the brothers. It was a military style facility, and although Duke was like a drill sergeant, Stone had a whole staff of military personnel.

A general curriculum was taught (math, social studies, reading, writing, physical education, history, etc.), in addition to religious instruction. Mean Mrs. Greenly, the school principal, was a stern authoritarian and didn't stand for any foolishness from the children. She was a short, stout, sallow-skinned white woman with a huge red beehive hairdo, adding another ten inches to her five-foot frame. She wore sensible, tan marshmallow shoes and tiny brown cat eyeglasses, which sat so far inside her eye sockets (and right up against her eyes) so that when she turned sideways you couldn't see the glasses at all. The arms of the frames swung back low and seemed to miraculously hang onto her ears. Mrs. Greenly especially concerned herself with the organization and strict supervision of off-premises trips to the Botanical Gardens, museums, the circus and Central Park, mainly because both girls and the boys would attend these trips. Girls were housed and schooled in separate parts of the building, so there wasn't much inter-mingling between "mischievous and sexually curious children."

When class trips were scheduled, the older boys took particular interest in their grooming habits, using whatever they had to freshen up for the girls. Breath fresh, hair combed, ears clean. Whatever it took for the girls to let them get close. Jimmy was only eight years old, so girls weren't his primary interest. Fighting and survival were most prevalent at the time.

Six months after Roy and Jimmy, another set of brothers arrived at the Center. Reginald and Trenton Clarke's parents lost their lives in a tragic car accident, and unfortunately they had no other family to care for them. Reggie was the same age as Jimmy and Reggie's older brother Trenton was eleven. At first, Reggie would tease Roy and Jimmy with all the other boys, but subsequently, he and Jimmy became great friends. They could always be found together, playing pranks and getting into trouble together. Having a close friend to confide in was a comfort to Jimmy, because he didn't have to pretend to be rough and tough all the time with his best friend.

In early spring, fourteen months after Jimmy and Roy were left on the steps of the Stone Center, Duke stopped in for a visit. As usual, he was looking dapper in a sharp gray suit, shiny black shoes, fancy tie with a piano print on it, crisp gray hat, and new gray overcoat. He smelled of fresh scented cologne and his hair and face were freshly shaven and trimmed. He was cleaner than Count Basie himself. Mrs. Greenly had Pops gather up the boys from their respective dormitories and brought them to the main office to see their father. Duke and the boys went up to the roof where they could be alone, have a nice visit and talk.

When they were outside and alone, a very angry Jimmy looked at Duke and asked, "Are you here to take us home?" "No son, I'm just in town briefly and I have to go back out on the road tomorrow," said Duke. A defeated and disappointed Jimmy frowned up his face and turned his back on Duke. "Don't you ever turn your back on me boy. I'll tear your head off." Jimmy fumed and walked over to the edge of the roof, threatening to jump. Duke looked at Jimmy, and with a voice like cold steel said, "Go ahead... jump."

Jimmy looked over the edge and down at the street, then looked back at Duke. He backed away from the edge into a safe area on the roof, but he wanted so badly to just jump if for nothing more than to show his father that he would actually do it. But, he didn't see the sense in killing himself to spite his father. Once his son was close enough, Duke grabbed Jimmy by the collar and beat him unmercifully. Roy quietly watched in tears as Duke wailed on his frail younger brother.

Later in the winter of that year, Duke stopped in for another visit. This time he brought his whole band to perform, a treat for the children. They set up their instruments on stage in the auditorium and put on a great show. They performed three numbers for the kids and Duke was a big hit. It was the first time most of the children had ever seen a vibraphone, and the kids loved it. Everybody cheered and told Jimmy and Roy their father was great. This gained points around the center for the boys. But, it didn't mean much to Jimmy. He would have preferred that his father take them to live with him rather than stop in and show off on stage. He knew that after the show, Duke would be gone.

The Andersons

Brenda: "While I was blessed with the Robinsons, Jimmy got stuck with The Andersons."

Jimmy and Roy lived at the center for two years. One day, Opal and Joseph Anderson came to John W. Stone Center for Orphans to adopt two boys. The Andersons were a middle-class black couple from St. Albans, Queens who had a teenaged daughter named Susan. Mainly, they needed a couple of strong, able-bodied boys to help around the house with chores and errands. Foster children in the sixties were a good, inexpensive way to meet this need, and make a bit of profit to boot.

Opal was both the brains and the muscle in the family and made all of the major decisions of the household. Joseph was a fairly quiet man who kept to himself, and didn't like problems. When Mrs. Greenly heard the Andersons were looking for two boys, she thought Jimmy and Roy could possibly be a good match. She arranged for the boys to be cleaned up and dressed in their best, and had them sent down to the intake room to meet the Andersons.

This get-together was more like a cattle sale than a meeting. They stood quietly as Mrs. Anderson pulled their bottom lips down and told them to smile so she could get a good look at their teeth. She told them to put their arms straight out in front of them, palms up, then turn them over, palm side down. She looked in their scalp to make sure their hair was clean and behind their ears. After inspection, they were sent back to their respective dorms. The boys were not asked any questions throughout this interview process. It was all decided between the prospective couple and Mrs. Greenly. Two days later, Jimmy and Roy were told to pack their bags.

Before children at the Stone Center were sent to their new foster homes, they were sent to a place called Lincoln Watts. It was a settlement of cottages in different areas of the city where orphans were sent for two or three days prior and taught how to behave in a private home. In essence, it was a program to teach kids manners and etiquette. Once again, Roy was placed in the same group of cottages with Jimmy, but not the same bungalow.

They separated the children by age groups, similar to the center. Seniors from the local colleges would head up and run each of the units, as they earned college credit and material for their thesis projects. The boys were taught general table manners and self-discipline. They learned how to behave at the dinner table and when to respond with yes ma'am and no sir, and the like. Jimmy and Roy, of course, had already been taught these things from their father. Nonetheless, they were required to go through the Lincoln Watts program as a formality.

The Andersons already had two foster sons there when Roy and Jimmy arrived. Rubin Parker and Alowishus "Jack" Jackson were their names, and they had come from a different children's facility in Queens. All of the boys slept in the tiny attic, but each of them had their own small bed. Opal had put two additional beds up in the attic of her home with a small table and tiny lamp with a low wattage light bulb that hardly gave off any light. Each boy was provided a few drawers for their clothes, and they all shared two closets. They were instructed to fold up any other clothing and stack them at the bottom of the closet for storage. Any additional items were to be stored under the beds in order to keep the attic tidy.

The family gave Jimmy the nickname "Pepi", and they always referred to him as such. The two new boys were each given a list of daily chores as the others had been given when they arrived, and any free time they had was to be spent studying or helping Joseph with his projects around the house. Joseph was pretty nice to the boys (especially when

Opal wasn't around) and he didn't treat them badly. In fact, he originally wanted the boys to call him Joe. However, the boys felt that was too informal and settled on Mr. Joe instead. Opal, on the other hand, was another matter entirely.

Opal was extremely cheap and did not spend a dime above what was required by the state to care for the boys. She would feed the boys the same meals every single day for the entire time they would live there. For breakfast, she would serve them thick, heavy oatmeal with Tip Top or Silvercup bread. Lunch was a peanut butter and jelly sandwich in a brown paper bag. It would always soak through the bag and be greasy by lunchtime. For dinner, it was white rice and corned beef every night. The only exception to this menu would be when Joseph, on occasion, would make bacon and eggs on Sunday and give that to the boys. It was their only treat, and they liked Mr. Joe for that alone. Opal would prepare completely separate and much tastier meals for her own family, but would keep the boys on their strict menu.

Mr. Joe especially took to Jimmy because he was always good with his hands. He could do everything he was asked and was a quick learner. Anytime Mr. Joe had a project to tackle, building a small shed, tooling with the car, hammering out some sheet metal, or spackling walls, Jimmy would be the one to help Mr. Joe out. Roy was fairly quiet, and stayed to himself most of the time.

Not surprisingly, Jimmy had many run-ins with Opal. He was headstrong, and would throw things a lot. He was always in trouble. She was pretty mean and feisty, which made for a bad combination. He didn't like her because she was mean and treated him and Roy with very little regard, no matter how good they were. She was never interested in being a mother or nurturer to them. She had very few kind words for them. She made her position in their lives clear from the beginning.

Opal would often badmouth Duke to the boys, and this infuriated Jimmy. He didn't like nor allow anyone to talk about his dad. No matter how badly he treated them. Susan, the Andersons' daughter, was more like her father than her mother. She was always nice and kind to the boys. Susan was studying to be an x-ray technician, and would later get a job in one of the local hospitals. It was a really good job with great pay and benefits, and her parents were proud of her, although Opal didn't show it much. Susan's choice of occupation and training would prove purposeful.

One day Jimmy was playing football with some of the neighborhood boys in St. Albans Park, not far from the Anderson home. He went up to catch a long pass and came down on his left knee, tearing a ligament, and immediately passed out. When the other boys saw that he was unconscious, they ran off and left him there. They feared he was dead and didn't want to be implicated. When he came to, the park was empty and he was alone. He rose to his feet and could hardly walk. So, he hopped all the way home and went up to his room without saying a word.

The next day, he woke up to a tremendous pain in his side. He doubled over onto the floor and began screaming. Susan was the only one home besides Jimmy and she came running upstairs to the attic. After quickly and calmly surveying the situation, Susan realized Jimmy's appendix had burst and immediately called an ambulance to the house. They were rushed to Queens General Hospital where doctors performed emergency surgery. As doctors pumped the poison out of his body, Jimmy thought he was dying. When he awoke in recovery, Susan was right there by his side. Jimmy always credited her for saving his life. If not for her quick thinking, he would most certainly have died that day.

Throughout their time at the Andersons, Duke sent the boys cards, letters and even coins from other countries. But, he would visit them only twice. Both times when he was on his way to visit, Jimmy somehow knew he was coming. He told Roy out of the blue, "Dad is coming to town. He'll be here in two days."

"How do you know that?"

"I just know."

And sure enough, Duke would show up at the Anderson's door. He could somehow sense him. It was a connection he would hate as a child, and somber over as an adult.

The first time Duke came, he took the boys outside and over to a neighborhood store to buy them a soda and candy. It was a real mom and pop store, and 'mom' was up on a ladder behind the counter stocking supplies, while 'pop' was in the back taking inventory. When she heard them come in, she didn't turn around, but just yelled out, "Be right with ya."

The boys looked around and eyed their selections, but didn't touch anything until Duke said it was okay to do so. After five minutes, Duke went over to the ladder and yelled for the lady to get down and help them immediately. The woman whirled around and nearly broke her neck, falling off the ladder. 'Pop' came out from the back to help his wife out and asked what was going on. Duke proceeded to get into an argument with the man, and eventually the three of them were kicked out of the store. Duke cursed the man, his wife, and their store. Needless to say, the boys got no treats that day.

The second time, Duke was in town for a few days and came to visit the boys. Mr. Joe's car had disappeared from in front of the house. Duke, being suspicious of everything and everyone, was quick to accuse the boys who lived in Opal & Joe's house, including his own sons. There was no basis for his accusations. A hundred other things could have happened to the car. It was almost as if he couldn't imagine there being a more rational explanation. For him, it was simply unruly boys misbehaving. "It was probably those boys, up to no good. I wouldn't stand for that" he told Opal. She just stared at him arms folded without saying a word, because she knew there was a good chance Joe's car had actually been repossessed for unpaid parking tickets. As far as she was concerned it was her house and she would decide what discipline is doled out to whom.

A Noble Chan

Jimmy had several odd jobs when he was in junior high school. He had a newspaper route. He would bag groceries at the supermarket, mow lawns, and work at the local drug store delivering medicine. It would have been a good way for Jimmy to save up a little money, if not for Opal's insistence on him handing over his earnings every time he got paid. This left him with barely anything to spend or save. If he protested, she would remind him that she paid for his clothes and gave him and his brother a place to sleep.

When Jimmy was in his sophomore and junior years at Woodrow Wilson High School (now known as August Martin High School), the most infamous gang in Jamaica, Queens were the Chaplins, also well known throughout the five boroughs. There were also the El Quentos, the Mohicans, and the Counts, just to name a few.

Jimmy joined a gang called the Noble Chans during his sophomore and junior years at Wilson. An offshoot of the Chaplins, there were about ten members. All the Chans wore the same outfits: navy blue bell bottom pants, white turtleneck shirts, suspenders, and white bucks on their feet. The gang originated in school, and like most gangs, provided a brotherhood for the boys in the neighborhood.

Jimmy was selected because he seemed troublesome and could certainly hold his own in a fight. In the 50's, it was a rare occurrence to hear of someone getting shot. Gang members used chains, pipes, sticks, zip guns to have all-out wars. They were real life West Side Story brawls minus all the dancing and finger snapping. Many of these brawls would take place in St. Albans Park or Baisley Park. Gangs would also claim certain floors or areas in local schools, and dare anyone to overstep their boundaries. The Noble Chans chased off members of rival gangs if they were seen on the second floor of the school. They had their turf 'on lock'.

Although Jimmy was a dedicated member of the Noble Chans, he was a smart student and performed fairly well in his second and third year of high school. At the prompting of a teacher who told him he had serious potential, Jimmy took up commercial arts in school. He excelled in the class, and would have given it serious consideration for a career in the future. Unfortunately, the classes were held up on the *third* floor. Rival gang members would chase Jimmy off the floor, making it almost impossible for him to attend the classes.

All the kids in the neighborhood used to walk to school. And there weren't as many private homes set close together in St. Albans then. It was a very wide-open space for the most part. So, in the winter, it was an extremely windy and bitter cold trek to and from school. Since most kids Jimmy went to school with were very poor, they wore what they could to keep warm. Jimmy and the other Noble Chans couldn't afford gloves or hats, so they wore socks on their hands and stocking caps made from women's pantyhose on their heads. Opal would give Jimmy her old stockings she was about to throw out, and he would tie a knot at the top and wear that on his head until it ripped, or got such a large run in it his head would be exposed, rendering it useless. It was better than freezing.

Once, Jimmy had a run-in with a big bully at school, at least twice Jimmy's size. His name was George Marshall. George was the kind of bully that would go around punching people in the back and then dare them to fight him. Most people were afraid of him, so he got away with it most times. One day as Jimmy walked in to the school, George punched Jimmy square in the back, then turned around to go up to the third floor. Jimmy balled his fists, turned around and punched George hard in his back. Seeing a teacher was watching from down the hall, George turned to Jimmy and said in a low voice "I'm gonna get you."

Before the school day was over, Jimmy told a couple of his boys that he was going to fight George after school, but off the school premises to avoid getting expelled. From the time he walked out of school and all the way down Parsons Boulevard with the crowd, he had been 'woofing' about how he was going kick George's ass. He wasn't afraid at all. He'd gone up against bigger boys at Stone Center, Opal and his own father. He just didn't want it to go too far… just enough to stop the bullying and let George know the Noble Chans meant business.

His plan was to get some good, hard punches in, then his boys would jump in and rough George up a little more. That day it was supposed to rain. Jimmy was carrying a tall umbrella with a steel tip on it. He thought 'If things get out of control, I'll stab this fool with the umbrella.'

When the crowd got to Parsons, he looked around and his boys were nowhere to be found. He had been talking trash and entertaining the other kids, and hardly noticed his boys weren't there. They had deserted him. Being forced now to face the bully alone, Jimmy jumped up in his face in front of everybody, took the steel-tip umbrella and stabbed him in the back twice, then jumped on the bus, just as it was taking off down Parsons Boulevard.

Jimmy thought he may have killed George, and was running for his life. He didn't know whether he was dead or alive. He just went home and prayed the police wouldn't come knocking on Opal and Mr. Joe's front door. The next day when he got to school, George was outside with a uniformed police officer, his father, and a black undercover police officer. He pointed Jimmy out to the police. They called him over and questioned him about the incident. Jimmy admitted to stabbing the bully in the back, but added that the kid was bullying him and that he does this to all the kids at school, too. So, he was really defending himself. The boy's father looked perplexed and shouted, "Are you crazy?" He couldn't believe that a kid could stab another kid in the back and walk away with no regard for his health or knowledge of whether he was dead or not. Granted, it was a pretty crazy thing to do. But, Jimmy felt he didn't have any choice in the situation. And that would be impossible to explain to the bully's father, or better yet, to the police. Just then, a teacher raced out of the front door, and down the steps of the school. She had heard about the fight, and had seen the police outside waiting with George's entourage. She figured they were waiting for Jimmy to arrive, and would certainly cart him off to jail. "What is going on here?!" When they confirmed what had happened the day before, she explained this was the result of George's bullying and she defended Jimmy's actions. She is the only reason Jimmy wasn't thrown into juvenile detention.

In Jimmy's senior year, he acquired a used car. He and his buddy Ron were out one day and parked the car in their neighborhood. When they returned to the car, they saw broken glass on the sidewalk and a guy leaning half-way into the car. He was rifling through the glove compartment when Jimmy and his friend rolled up on him. The guy was so startled, he dropped the stolen items on the ground. Jimmy grabbed the thief, threw him up against the side of the car and said, "You were gonna rob ME?!" Ron pulled out a gun and held it to the thief's side with a half-mad, half-crazed look on his face. Jimmy grabbed the gun from his friend. "What the hell is wrong with you? Are you crazy?"

Ron looked surprised, but kept his eye on the thief. Jimmy looked around, then put the gun in his pocket. He grabbed the guy by the collar and shook him. Then he threatened him, saying that the three of them were going to walk down the block to the police station and the thief was going to confess. Jimmy practically dragged him down the block and into the police station. As small as he was, people were afraid of the rage that was in his eyes. It wasn't until Jimmy and Ron left the police station did they realize that they could have been arrested for having an illegal gun.

Despite all the missed work in his Art class, Jimmy's teacher recognized his raw talent and anonymously entered Jimmy's work into a contest. To his credit, Jimmy won a certificate for Commercial Arts and a heavy gold medal that helped him get accepted into an art program at Hunter College in Manhattan. His art teacher had entered him into a contest, because he liked his work and believed Jimmy had great promise. He would remark that Jimmy could be a great architect or sketch artist. When Jimmy won the award, his teacher was thrilled and tried to give him as much encouragement as possible. But, the rival gangs would chase Jimmy away from the art floor once again. He never told the teacher why he wasn't going to the class. He simply shrugged off the class, and stopped going. He figured he would resume his interest in Art after high school. Maybe he'd get a job at a fancy gallery, or at one of the big museums in Manhattan. It would have been nice to tell his teacher the truth, maybe he could have helped in some way. But, Jimmy didn't trust him, or anyone else except Roy and his crew.

Jimmy reached a critical turning point in his life during his senior year at Wilson. It was Thanksgiving, and three members of his gang were planning to rob a local drug store. Ordinarily, Jimmy would have gone with them. Not because he wanted to rob or hurt anyone. Really, Jimmy was no criminal. But, on this day, fate stepped in. Jimmy and Ron skipped the robbery to visit a couple of girls that night in their neighborhood. They hung out with the girls for a few hours, then they both went home afterwards. The next day Jimmy and Ron heard that the robbery had gone bad, and their fellow gang members had been arrested for killing the store clerk. The clerk had apparently put up a fight and someone shot him. Jimmy took this as a sign, and soon after that, he went straight. Some years later, Jimmy heard that the shooter was sentenced to death by electric chair. Maybe it was intuition. Or maybe it was God's divine intervention. But, Jimmy quit the gang and got a part-time job to fill up his spare time. It kept him out of trouble, and he went on to graduate on time.

The Just 3

Roy had only been with the Chaplins' for a brief period of time while Jimmy was running with the Noble Chans. After he left, he enjoyed learning and teaching Latin dance locally. Roy was an excellent dancer and was a favorite at the famous Palladium Theater in Manhattan. He and his friend Emerson were so good, they were hired by the Palladium to teach Latin dance on the weekends. Dance would continue to be Roy's passion. He competed in local competitions, and later on professionally. He even won titles around the Tri-State in Latin dance.

Opal had already been taking the greater portion of Roy's earnings, and had been demanding a portion of Jimmy's, too. He knew he couldn't move out until he was 18, and had to give her money at least until then. On February 5, 1957, his 17th birthday, Opal ordered him to hand over his whole paycheck. She accused him of holding out and used her leverage of owning him until he was 18 over his head. But Jimmy was fed up and refused to give her another dime of the money he earned. "Where's my money?" she demanded. He braced himself for a fight, stood as tall as he could "That's my money and I'm not giving you any more of it. I earned it!" he protested. Seething, Opal balling her fists, stared him down "Oh, you think this is free?! This is not free. Not any of it. There is a cost to pay when you live in someone else's house, ungrateful little bastard." Jimmy was silent, and unwavering. He was ready for this stand-off, and he would not back down. Not for Duke, and certainly not for her. Opal went on, "I give you a place to lay your head, food in your belly, and treat you like a member of my family, and your selfish little ass..." Jimmy interrupted, "I'm not giving you a dime," and he meant it. Roy was already forking over his check to Opal without any complaints, and she expected the same from Jimmy. But, Jimmy was determined to keep his hard-earned dollars for himself. Jimmy knew he could not stay there any longer. So, he packed his meager belongings and left the Andersons for good. He had nowhere to go, but he was determined to keep Opal from stealing his money. He lived out of his tiny car for weeks. Nonetheless, he woke up early every single morning and arrived to work on time. He showered at the local YMCA, which was free and open to the public, and washed his clothes at the laundromat. In the evenings, he hung out with his buddies and sung in small, local talent shows. They went to parties and met girls, and they all had a great time. It wasn't always easy living out of his car, but Jimmy had never felt so free.

One evening, Jimmy's buddy Merlin told him about a free party a friend was throwing at the skating rink. He said everyone was going to be there, and that Jimmy should throw on his 'best rags' and meet him there.

Jimmy went to his car and pulled out white pants, white short-sleeve button down shirt, black skinny belt, black socks and a pair of white skips. He took the bundle down to the laundromat where Ms. Lou let him use her iron. He changed in the restroom, slicked his short, black hair to one side, stood back and admired himself in the full-length mirror, then headed over to the skate party.

The rink was slowly getting crowded, but Jimmy quickly found Merlin by the snack area where he stopped to buy himself a cola.

Brenda was at the counter giving her shoe size to the attendant with her friends Donna, Joanne, and Pat. She was a junior at John Adams High School at the time, and quite the tomboy. Jimmy had seen her before around the neighborhood, but didn't know her very well. She had on a red and black plaid coat that she wore all the time, a long red skirt and black and white bucks on her feet. It wasn't until she finally parted with her favorite coat halfway through the party that Jimmy realized she was actually quite shapely.

They all skated and danced and sat around talking after the party, and Jimmy found out that Brenda not only had a soft side, but she had a great voice and was an exceptional singer.

Brenda and Jimmy discovered they both loved all the doo-wop greats. They practiced singing songs together, including The Moonglows' 'The Ten Commandments of Love', 'I'm So Young' by The Students, 'The Great Pretender' and 'Smoke Gets in Your Eyes' by The Platters. Jimmy formed a group called Vicky & The Concepts. The group was made up of Jimmy, a guy named Syd Washington, and Brenda sang lead. Jimmy wrote the songs, coordinated the outfits, and set up the shows for them to perform around town. Their sound was not unlike other similar styled groups, but they did sound sweet together. Jimmy could sing first tenor, second tenor and even baritone. Coupled with Brenda's alto lead, they had a show-stopping sound. With Jimmy hustling aggressively on behalf of the group, Brenda became both excited and hopeful that she could be a great female lead singer.

Jimmy shared with Brenda that he'd been physically and emotionally abused by his father. He told her all about growing up in the shelter and later being placed into foster care. He explained he experienced a lot of hardships, and told her about his older brother and promised to introduce her to his best friend Reggie who was like a brother to him. He always had Reggie as a confidante. But, as he got to know Brenda he began to let his guard down with her, and share more about himself. She could relate to his struggles as a child, his loneliness, and his continued search for love and acceptance. She developed a trust in him that made her feel safe and loved as well. Brenda and Jimmy became inseparable by late 1958, and kept singing around town whenever they could get bookings.

Jimmy continued to work a steady job between singing performances, but wasn't making much money. He lived alone in the basement of a friend's uncle's house off Linden Boulevard, paying $10 a week for rent. This left only few extra dollars to spend on the group's expenses. Unfortunately, the landlord needed the apartment for a relative returning from North Carolina and told Jimmy he had to move out by the end of the week. With nowhere else to go, Brenda brought Jimmy to Kate and Dave and asked if he could live in the basement. Reluctantly, they agreed. Brenda had never shown much interest in boys before. So, Kate wanted to keep a close eye on the two of them.

Vicky & The Concepts rehearsed almost daily in the basement to get ready for their shows. Syd Washington went off to the army, which left the group without a second male voice. So, another guy named Donald

German joined the group, and Jimmy changed the name of the group to The Just 3. Jimmy had been approached by James Dailey, manager/promoter of a very popular girl-group at the time. Their hit record was a catchy, upbeat tune written about Dailey. He told Jimmy he could use his many connections to make The Just 3 'hot' like his girl group. In late 1959 and into the middle of 1960, The Just 3 recorded three songs written by Jimmy, 'Bad Girl', 'When You Love You Lose' and 'Cry, Cry'. Their big local hit was 'You Ain't No Friend Of Mine', which they recorded and pressed in March 1960. Dailey got them an audition with Decker Records in Manhattan, and arranged for them to lay down tracks in the studio. Jimmy and Brenda were excited that they were finally on their way.

The first day in the studio, Brenda was extremely nervous and took hours to adjust to being in a real recording studio. She sang too low at first, and had trouble projecting her voice as Jimmy coached her from inside the control booth. Jimmy asked the engineer to stop recording and he went inside to talk to her.

"I'm sorry," Brenda whispered to Jimmy.

"Look, we only have one shot at this. This is the big time, Brenda. You have to go for it."

Brenda paused, took a deep breath, and said she could do it. She was ready. From the booth, Jimmy cued Brenda to get ready again. When the music was keyed back up and the first rift came in Brenda belted out that first verse with the power and confidence of a seasoned professional. Jimmy couldn't believe what he was hearing. Her voice rivaled the best singers of the time. They laid down the entire track that day, and the record was pressed in a week. Mr. Dailey was thrilled with the songs and their sound, and promised to push the group full speed ahead. The members of The Just 3 were so excited, they started dreaming and making plans for the future. The record executives at Decker also liked the group's sound, but wanted to change some of the lyrics in Jimmy's songs. Jimmy and Brenda were ready to agree to the changes, but Dailey flatly refused to change anything. He told them he was the best promoter and manager in the business, and that The Just 3 were too good for the deal they were being offered. As a result, no one wanted to work with him, and Decker dropped The Just 3 cold. Jimmy went to Dailey's house weeks later and was only able to recover one of his masters. Days later, Dailey was nowhere to be found. He had disappeared, along with the masters. Jimmy never got them back. He couldn't afford to fight in court. He tried to get another promoter or manager to help The Just 3 get off the ground, but he was never able to find anyone reputable that would get behind the group. The Just 3 performed locally at dances and birthday parties, but, like lots of groups of their generation, they wouldn't find the success they had dreamed of.

Rock-A-Bye Baby

By the end of 1960, The Shirelles had released 'Dedicated' and 'Tonight's The Night', and Brenda had just discovered she was pregnant. She was deathly afraid to tell Kate and Dave.

The first person she called, even before she told Jimmy, was Donna. Donna came over to Brenda's house and they locked themselves in the basement trying to figure out what Brenda should do. Donna said she had heard that there were people who could get rid of babies. She made a few calls and got the information. They both walked to a drug store outside of their neighborhood and purchased some white pills that were supposed to make a girl's period come down. The pills only made Brenda violently sick. She threw up for hours, but no period came down and she was still pregnant. From another friend they had heard you could take boiled turpentine, put it in a metal bucket and sit on it, and that was supposed to draw out the fetus. Brenda locked the basement door, they boiled the turpentine on the basement stove, and she squatted over the silver, metal bucket for over an hour. The fumes from the hot turpentine made her dizzy and nauseous, and after the first ten minutes her skin began to burn. She vomited and had a terrible headache afterwards, and her butt and thighs were chaffed and red from the hot solution. She finally gave up and went next door to tell their neighbor, Ms. Tina, to see if she could help her. Tina said, "I knew something was wrong with you." "How am I gonna tell mom and dad, Ms. Tina?" Brenda pleaded. She said, "Ok, here's what we'll do... I'll go over there first and take some liquor, to ease them into it. Louis (her husband) will take Dave and I'll take Kate. You just stay upstairs and wait."

Brenda was upstairs pacing back and forth, wringing her hands, worried to death when Tina and Louis arrived with the liquor in hand. She was too nervous to peek down the stairs, but she listened as closely as she could from her room. Tina kept Kate talking and laughing the whole time, but she occasionally looked up at the creaking ceiling because Brenda kept pacing back and forth. After Tina and Louis left Kate went straight upstairs. She walked into Brenda's room and said, "What's wrong with you?" Brenda looked down, "Nothing." "I know something's wrong, so you may as well come clean now," said Kate. From downstairs all Dave heard was, "ARE YOU CRAZY! WHAT IN THE HELL IS WRONG WITH YOU? ARE YOU STUPID OR SOMETHING?!" Dave came running upstairs, "What's wrong, what happened?" "Your daughter's pregnant, THAT'S what happened!"

Brenda was silent. She couldn't say anything. She couldn't defend herself. She knew better than to open her mouth because it would only make things worse. So, she took the verbal bashing. She was more concerned that Dave would kill Jimmy. Jimmy was downstairs in the basement, also waiting for the fur to fly. He heard Dave heading down the basement steps and he backed up to brace himself for whatever was coming. He knew he might have to fight Dave, so he hid a heavy wooden baseball bat in the corner where he was standing, just in case. He looked at Jimmy and said, "I let you live in my basement out of the kindness of my heart and this is how you repay me? You go and knock my daughter up??? Get upstairs right now." Jimmy breathed a small breath and followed Dave upstairs looking behind him at the bat still in the corner.

In the living room both Brenda and Jimmy were sitting far away from each other on the couch. Dave and Kate were screaming at the top of their lungs, shouting questions and orders at them so fast neither one of them could respond, nor did they want to. Dave called Jimmy ungrateful and threatened to kill him. Kate was angry and upset, but calmed down and said to Brenda, "So, what do you think you're gonna do now, huh? You haven't even graduated from high school yet?! And Jimmy, what are you gonna do?" Dave interrupted, "Oh, I know what he's GONNA do... he's gonna marry my daughter, that's what he's gonna do!" Kate agreed and said, "You two are not embarrassing us. You are definitely getting married." Jimmy looked up at Kate and Dave, eyes pleading, "But, I'm too young to get married." Dave looked like a crazed lunatic now. "What... what did you say?" He never waited for Jimmy's response. "You ARE gonna MARRY her, period, end of story." Jimmy and Brenda looked at one another and both put their heads down, Jimmy visualizing his music career slipping away, and Brenda too ashamed to protest or look up at either parent. And just like that plans were made for the wedding of Jimmy and Brenda.

Jimmy had reassured Brenda he would stick by her, and take care of his responsibilities. When they first met, he shared with Brenda that his father was not there for him, and that he would never abandon his children the way his father did.

Jimmy and Brenda were married in Kate and Dave's living room on January 20, 1959, when Brenda was 17 and Jimmy was 19. Kate's pastor, Reverend Boyd, Donna and Joanne, Jimmy's best friend Reggie, and some of Dave and Kate's immediate family, including Dill and Alice were present. Donna's mother made the simple white wedding dress on her big Singer sewing machine. Kate roasted a chicken, whipped up some collards and potato salad, and baked a fresh apple pie, Brenda's favorite. It was an uncomfortable couple of hours, and after everyone left Jimmy and Brenda took a cab to Manhattan and checked into The Hilton Hotel for two nights. While there they did things they thought they were supposed to do as a married couple, but mainly they just watched TV, and ate food and snacks. Brenda took the time to have a talk with Jimmy about their future. She expressed her disappointment that they had to get married under the circumstances, and she said she knew they were both not ready for all of the things they were about to get into. However, she acknowledged that as friends they had to always be honest with one another and she hoped they would continue to be honest. She said, "If at any time you decide you don't want to be in this marriage with me, please come and talk to me. Just please don't lie to me." Jimmy agreed.

As Brenda's belly grew, she had no choice but to drop out of high school. Jimmy worked his full-time job to get things in order for the arrival of the baby, and Dave was still mad as hell about the entire situation. Brenda and Jimmy wanted to continue performing to make extra money, but Brenda's belly was so big now and no one wanted to see a pregnant lead singer on stage. She and Jimmy agreed she would take the break to rest up for the final stretch of the pregnancy. On April

29, 1961, Brenda gave birth to baby girl, Sabrina. She insisted that Donna be appointed the godmother. Brenda and Sabrina moved down into the basement with Jimmy, and Jimmy stayed out of Dave's way.

One evening several months later, all hell broke loose. Brenda had just finished feeding and bathing Sabrina, and was putting her down for a nap in her bassinet when Dave stumbled into the house. He had been out drinking, and as it happened often in these situations, Dave had soiled his trousers with urine. He walked in slowly and steadily, trying hard not to stumble, and was about to sit down on Kate's nice couches. Kate entered the den wiping the yellow, mayonnaise-y potato salad remnants from her hands onto her red and white-checkered dish drying rag, "DAVID! Don't you sit your pissy behind on my couches!" Dave jumped up before his butt could hit the cushions, frowned and mumbled something unintelligible under his breath and was making his way upstairs. She rolled her eyes, pursed her lips tight, and returned to the kitchen to finish dinner. She peeked her head out yelling "… And make sure you take off those pants and wash up."

He started raising hell, cursing loud and shouting. Sabrina woke up and began crying and screaming. Dave picked up the baby and started kissing and hugging her, all the while she's hollering. Brenda, now pregnant with her second child and being very careful because of it, calmly tried to take the baby from him. He snatched the baby away saying, "Oh, I can't hold the mother fuckin' baby now?! What kind of shit is going on around here?!" He smooched the baby, "Even if she 'aint named after me… it's still my mother fuckin' house." Brenda could see the situation was out of control and asked him to give her the baby. Dave refused, sat down on Kate's small chaise lounge in the corner of the bedroom and began bouncing Sabrina up and down on his knee. Jimmy heard all the commotion and came upstairs to see what was going on. He entered the room, seeing the baby's head flopping back and forth and freaked out. He raced over and tried unsuccessfully to snatch Sabrina from Dave. He got up in his face and threatening him, which only escalated matters, "What are you doing?!" "Don't you try to take my granddaughter from me! Who the hell do you think you are?" Holding the screaming baby away from her father, and staring fire at Jimmy, "You a MAN now??!" Kate entered the room and told everybody to, "Shut the hell up" which was the only curse word Brenda had ever heard her say. She yelled at Dave for causing the problem in the first place. Brenda finally got the baby away from Dave while she could and took her downstairs. Jimmy threatened Dave, "Don't you EVER touch my baby again!" Dave shot back, "And YOU can get the FUCK out of my house!" Seething, Jimmy stormed out the house and walked across the street, cut through the empty lot, which led him out to Farmers Boulevard. He was hot, and he knew he needed to calm down and catch his breath. He leaned against the brick wall on the side of the butcher shop, and took a few minutes to think about what he was going to do next. He had never seen Dave so mad, not even when he and Brenda first told him she was pregnant. Things had gone too far this time.

A few seconds later he heard a car engine revving up. He turned around to see Dave behind the wheel of his 1957 aqua blue Chevy Bel-Air coming at him fast. Jimmy jumped out of the path of the vehicle just in time for Dave to zoom by him and slam his car head-on into a tree. Dazed but not injured, Dave stuck his head out of the window, "I'M GONNA KILL YOU Jimmy!" Jimmy ran at top speed around the corner and headed to his friend Ray's house where he could lay low for a few days.

Who's Foolin' Who

Jimmy and Brenda moved out of Kate and Dave's house two days later, taking furniture and all necessary personal belongings. They moved around the corner into a basement apartment of a house where Kate's friend Zella was both a tenant and the superintendent. They lived in that apartment for only a few months, but as the winter approached the basement was too cold and damp for baby Sabrina seeing she kept catching colds. So, they moved out of the basement and into a one-bedroom apartment on Merrick Boulevard, near Baisley Boulevard.

They began experiencing problems in their relationship early on. Being such a young couple, with very little support and Brenda close to giving birth to their second child, Brenda decided it would be best for her and Sabrina to move back home with Kate and Dave. She could be close to her mother, and get the support she and her children needed. On May 4, 1962, Brenda gave birth to another baby girl, and named her Cheresse. Jimmy came to visit the babies nearly every day and gave Brenda whatever money he made to care for them. Jimmy and Brenda separated and got back together and separated again until they had two more daughters, Karla and Summer, and secured a NYC Housing Authority home to rent in South Ozone Park, Queens.

By 1968, Brenda, Jimmy and their four daughters moved into the two-story, three-bedroom house. It was a quiet neighborhood with lots of kids. The house was a new attached home on 147th Street with parquet floors and a finished basement.

Jimmy had always worked a lot to provide for his family. But, now he was working many more hours and was sometimes required to travel upstate, which often kept him away from home. Brenda was spending most of her days caring for the girls, which left no time for singing or hanging out with friends, or even building a strong marriage. Joanne and Donna had visited a few times, but the visits turned into quick telephone calls where they would catch up – mainly Brenda talking about marriage and babies, and her girlfriends talking about careers and future plans. They were busy making travel plans, and moving on to greater, more promising things, and Brenda was genuinely happy for them. But it also left her feeling isolated and depressed.

She kept in touch with her sister Marilyn, and they saw each other occasionally. Marilyn sometimes visited late in the evenings after the kids were asleep, and she would always bring friends. They would all sit around drinking beer and wine, and some of her friends even smoked marijuana. Brenda had never done it before, but she was curious about the way the other ladies seemed so happy and relaxed after they smoked. She decided she was a grown woman now, so she asked Marilyn if she could try some 'reefer.' The first time she tried it she took a very long drag on the joint and burned her throat. She coughed for an hour straight, even water couldn't wash away the scorched sensation. She didn't understand how anyone would want to do that more than once. Marilyn's friend Lyn came into the kitchen where Brenda was trying to catch her breath and explained she had to take shorter 'pulls' off of the joint. She let Brenda try it again, but this time she took a short, even breath inward, held it in her throat the way she had seen Lyn do it, then she exhaled slowly until all the smoke left her lungs, throat and mouth. Brenda immediately felt lighter, loose in her arms and legs, and her head felt very, very relaxed. She giggled and smiled at Lyn who smiled back at her approvingly. She returned to the party going on in the living room, sipped on a beer, and changed the record on the record player from Creedence Clearwater Revival's 'Proud Mary' to 'I Can't Get Next to You' by the Temptations. Brenda rocked side to side and sunk down into the couch, wondering what Jimmy would say if he came home at that moment. She didn't want to think about that now. She was enjoying the laughter of the women around her, she stared at Lyn and wondered what it would be like to kiss her lips, touch her round breasts, and kiss her neck. She did not say any of this out loud. These were personal thoughts and she was enjoying this new feeling of freedom and discovery.

When Brenda woke up the next morning, she had a terrible headache. She squinted her eyes and held her head as she removed the silver foiled wrapping from the Swanson's pancake and sausage TV dinners and placed them in the oven. She listened to the girls upstairs fighting over who would get to use the bathroom first, and wondered where the past eight years had gone. In that short period of time, she had dropped out of high school, gotten married, had four children and was now a housewife. She felt lonely and more unfulfilled than she ever had in her life. She wanted to talk with Jimmy about it, but she didn't think he would understand. He worked all the time and she didn't want to seem ungrateful for all he was doing to keep the bills paid and a roof over their heads. She couldn't confide in Kate, because she would remind her that she was the one who got pregnant at 17 years old and ruined her life. She talked to Marilyn who she knew loved her and wished the best for her, but it wasn't really fair to ask Marilyn because she didn't have any children, and she lived a completely different lifestyle than Brenda.

Brenda knew this was something she had to figure out on her own. But, right now she needed to get the girls fed, dressed and off to school and daycare.

By 1970 Brenda began to suspect that Jimmy was cheating. For the next few months, she went through his things after he left for work, checked his pockets, his drawers, on the insides of his shoes, and up in his side of the closet. She found some old letters from Reggie that were written to Jimmy while he was away in the military. She interpreted some of the things that Reggie wrote in these letters as code that Jimmy was interested in or already involved with other women. She had no real proof, but she believed that her women's intuition was accurate. Making matters worse Jimmy came home from work exhausted, and didn't want to have sex with her anymore. This was odd too because Jimmy was always ready and willing for sex. One evening she confronted him, and they got into a terrible fight. She accused him of cheating with a woman from his job, and he flatly denied it saying, "You're crazy. I'm working my ass off for this family and you are accusing me of something like this?!" Brenda folded her arms tightly across her chest, twisted her lips to the left side of her face, leaned in toward his face and said, "Hell yeah, because I know what I know." She pointed her finger at him, "I told you nine years ago, Jimmy, that if you

didn't want to be in this thing with me anymore you could come talk to

me and if we couldn't work it out we could go our separate ways!" He

fell silent, just staring at her for a moment. Time seemed suspended. He

glanced up the stairs toward the two bedrooms where his four daughters

were sleeping soundly. He couldn't speak. He couldn't flat out deny that

something was wrong. But, he also knew his marriage was falling apart

at the seams. He thought of his daughters now. He was sad for them, and

sad for himself. He wanted to be better than his father, and tried hard to

fit into the mold of husband to Brenda. They used to be such great

friends, and now they were spewing hate at one another and had grown

apart. He didn't feel he knew this woman in front of him anymore. He

felt resentful, and angry now; angry that her parents forced them to marry

too early, and angry that he didn't feel like a man in his own home

anymore. Brenda had become distant, and started spending more time

with her female friends than with him. He tried to convince himself that

his wife was just lonely at home while he worked overtime to pay the

bills. But, when he walked in one evening to find naked women passed

out underneath sheets across the living room floor, he was livid. He

moved toward her, responding to her accusing finger, "Well, what about

you? In here with naked women smoking pot and doing God only knows what in front of our kids when I'm not home?!" He was shaking, his

voice angry but measured. He had been afraid to bring it up for weeks.

She moved in toward him with her fists balled up, leaned in, and slapped

him hard flat across the left side of his face. He recoiled quickly and

grabbed a tight hold on her wrists to keep her from swinging again. She

was crying and calling him all kind of assholes and bastards. He wrestled

her to the floor and held her until she calmed down. He thought she had

just calmed down on her own, but then he caught a glimpse of some

shadows at the top of the stairs and he froze. All the commotion had

woken up the girls and they were sitting on the stairs in their long, flannel

nightgowns with their arms around their knees watching and crying.

Brenda sat up and propped her back against the legs of the sofa, wiping

the tears and sweat off of her forehead and cheeks with her shirt. Without

saying a word, Jimmy headed up the stairs, squeezing past his crying

children. He went into the bedroom and began packing clothes and other

belongings in a bag. Still fuming, Brenda got up, straightened her clothes

and grabbed Jimmy's car keys off of the small table in front of the house.

Sabrina and Cheresse quickly slipped down the stairs, pulled back the

curtains to see their mother's head buried in the trunk as she rummaged

through its contents. Each time she stood up she pulled out some article of clothing out, or a bag of something, or shoes. Her hair was standing straight up on her head and she looked completely disheveled.

Jimmy came downstairs holding a black suitcase overflowing with necessities in his left hand, and a large crate of albums and 8-track cartridges in his other hand. His two youngest daughters following close behind sat on the sofa. Jimmy asked the girls to come away from the window so he could talk to them. Huddled together with the girls Jimmy said, "Please don't cry, it's gonna be okay. Your mom and I are just not getting along right now. I have to leave for a while, but I'll be back to see you real soon. I promise." "I will never be too far away." They all cried together for a moment, but Jimmy knew he had to leave before Brenda came back inside. He refused to have his daughters see them fighting again. He hugged the girls tight saying, "I love you all" then grabbed his suitcase and walked out the door. Brenda had thrown his things out onto the street and sidewalk, and the neighbors were at the windows and doors watching the show. They were waiting for the big finish. Jimmy dropped his crate and bag as he approached, shouting, "What in the hell are you doing?!" She held up each item then threw it at him before they fell to the ground, "What's this huh?" She pulled a wrinkled white dress shirt from behind her back and held it up in his face, "This is damn sure not MY lipstick on your collar!" Jimmy paused for a second. Then he calmly picked up his bag and crate, put them in the backseat of his car, then got in and started the car. Brenda was on him. She pulled open his car door, "You aint takin' my music! It's mine too." He reached into the backseat, took half of the albums out of the crate, threw them into the street and closed the door. Brenda jumped in front of the car and leaned on the hood so he couldn't drive off. "Oh, so you don't even care now?" she shouted over the engine. He just stared at her, tears in her eyes, tears in his too. Time stood still over the humming of the engine. He looked back at the girls still watching in the window, then back at her. She saw the girls too. Then she quietly moved away from the car, and he slowly drove away.

Free

The separation was rough for everyone. Jimmy was sad that the marriage to Brenda did not work out, but most of all he was devastated at having to leave his daughters. The girls missed their daddy, and he missed them more than they could know.

Jimmy still had his job, but he had nowhere to live, and no options. Once again, he found himself sleeping in his car and heading to work after a shower at the Y. He kept up appearances at work, but he was miserable after 5pm quitting time. He worked and saved his money. When he had a little money saved, he slept at a rooming house in Astoria, Queens. Once he saved enough money, he moved to an apartment on Dillon Street off Atlantic Avenue in Brooklyn. He stayed there for only two weeks. He kept hearing some kind of rattling from behind the refrigerator. One day he decided to investigate further and discovered the entire apartment was infested with huge water bugs. He immediately moved out. He had to find a decent place that was suitable to bring his daughters for visits.

With Jimmy gone, Brenda had to figure out how to pay the rent, heat the house, keep the lights on, feed and clothe her children, pay for school and extracurricular activities, pay for their medical, dental, and eye care expenses. These were things that had always been taken care of for Brenda. She hadn't given all of it much thought until shortly after Jimmy drove away from the house for the last time. Sabrina, Cheresse and Karla were already attending St. Clements Catholic School, but Summer was only 3 years old and had been at home with Brenda. She had to find a job and an affordable daycare center for Summer. She had never had a job before and didn't know what she was qualified to do. She knew she could call Kate and Dave if things got desperate. But, she wanted to show them she could take care of herself. Although she had no idea *how* she would do it. Things had turned into a mess with Jimmy as it was, and she didn't want them to berate her for getting pregnant in the first place. She locked herself in her bedroom, laid on the bed, and looked up at the ceiling for hours. For a long time, she stared at the paint, sometimes at nothing, but mostly she cried. She truly didn't know what to do. She only knew that she had to pull herself together. She decided she was strong and had survived difficult situations. She knew that some girls she went to high school with had turned to public assistance now that they were single mothers. But, she knew Kate would frown upon it. No one in Kate's family had ever had it so hard they'd turned to public assistance. They worked a job, brought home a paycheck, and took care of their families. She could not tell Kate all that was happening, not before trying to work it out herself. Brenda figured 'If anyone were qualified for it now, it would be her and four hungry, fatherless kids'. She didn't know if Jimmy would give her money for the kids or not, but she wasn't going to wait for that. And she didn't want to need him anymore. She decided she was going to do it on her own, without him, and without Kate and Dave. She would check with friends about how to apply for public assistance, and she would check the help wanted section of the newspaper.

She filed for public assistance but was unable to collect because she was only separated from Jimmy, not divorced and solely dependent on only Jimmy's income. She was told she had to wait a year until her divorce was final. So, for close to one year she sucked it up and let her parents help her financially.

When she finally did receive assistance, she got the maximum benefits allowed for a single mother with four children at that time: $400 per month, a $210 stipend for food and miscellaneous expenses, plus $190 to cover her portion of rent for the Section 8 house she was renting.

She received low-income medical insurance, which at least covered the basic medical, dental and vision plans for all four kids and herself. She hadn't planned to stay on public assistance at all. She was just biding her time until she could figure out what to do, and find a job. She refused to take Jimmy to court, because she didn't want his assistance, or his input on raising the kids.

Even with public assistance, she was barely able to pay the bills. She didn't know anything about managing a household budget, or about saving money. She didn't even have a bank account. It had been 13 months since Jimmy left. She didn't know where he was or what he was doing. Jimmy had actually called the girls nearly every day since he left, but he swore the girls to secrecy. Brenda figured he was probably with his new girlfriend, living it up and moving on, while she was overwhelmed and taking care of THEIR responsibilities. She resented him completely. They had vowed to be in this thing together, and now he was gone. She assumed he was sad because she knew he loved and missed his daughters, but she was primarily angry that he got to go and live his life like a free and single man, and she was stuck raising kids. 'Stuck' with her girls, because she would not have allowed Jimmy, or Kate and Dave, or anyone else to raise them. Not after she had been given away by her own parents, and left with another family to raise her. She cursed Jimmy for cheating, and breaking their vow to stick it out together, and to be honest with one another. The more she thought about it, the more it made sense to her that she couldn't just stay on public assistance and struggle alone. She had to seek financial support from her soon-to-be ex-husband. She filed the court papers, and asked the court to petition Jimmy to provide support for his daughters. Unfortunately, Jimmy was not earning much money of his own, and was apparently living out of his car for quite a while. When Brenda discovered this, it made her sad and she thought about letting him come back home. But, she knew it would be a disaster. Their marriage was done. Bringing him back would not give her the freedom she was becoming accustomed to, and it would only confuse the girls. The court ordered Jimmy to pay Brenda so little, approximately $50 per month, that it didn't make much sense to pursue it further. She dropped the case, and decided to make a go of it on her own.

From the time Brenda was a small child, she never learned much about cooking and preparing meals for a family. So, she lacked the skills to prepare home cooked meals for her daughters. Jimmy was a fairly decent cook, having had to prepare his own meals in the absence of parental guidance. So, when he and Brenda began living together, he did most of the cooking. Brenda's strength was cleaning and keeping order in the house. She was the disciplinarian, and he had worked and brought home his paychecks.

Brenda struggled daily to come up with creative meals the girls would actually eat. Breakfast was a snap: scrambled eggs, bacon, toast, French toast, pancakes, hot cereal, and cold cereal. All fairly cheap meals she could stretch, and the kids loved it. Lunches were canned soup and crackers, or sandwiches (bologna, liverwurst or tuna on a good day). Dinners were a bit trickier. She tried in vain to prepare chicken legs or liver, an inexpensive chicken alternative with thick, dry mashed potatoes or Kraft macaroni and cheese. But, she was terrible at it all, often under-seasoning the meat, and then over-cooking it to a crisp or undercooking it where it would still be pink or bloody inside. When this occurred, the girls would silently protest, but somehow 'get it down' since they knew there was nothing else to eat. They all compromised and Brenda bought Swanson tv dinners, which included a meat, a vegetable, a starch, and a dessert, all in a silver tray that popped right into the oven. The favorite was the Salisbury steak dinner, or the fried chicken dinner, which came with a tiny, doughy chocolate cake square in the middle. The girls would fight over who got which tv dinner. Once Brenda taught the older girls how to work the oven without burning down the house, everyone was happy.

Kate had taught Brenda how to thoroughly clean a house since she was a small child, living by the mantra that "...cleanliness was next to Godliness." So, she walked around the house picking up clothes, toys, books, towels, hair ribbons, crayons, and put everything in their proper order. She swept the floors, and used a bucket of hot, soapy water to scrub the kitchen and bathroom fixtures, walls and floors by hand. She would hit the kitchen first, clear off and polish the dining room table, beat the cushions of the living room couch, then make her way upstairs to clean the two girls' rooms, the bathroom and end with her own bedroom. She would head back downstairs and flop down exhausted on the couch, look around the room and think, "I may be poor, but at least I have a house." It was completely quiet, and she thought she could use a beer.

Dee Josephs

In 1971, Satchel Paige became the first African-American player to be inducted into the baseball Hall of Fame, Stevie Wonder released his album 'Where I'm Coming From," and President Nixon implemented a 90-day freeze on wages and prices in an attempt to control inflation. The climate in America was one of protest, anger and frustration, but there was also a strong determination in America for a better future in the coming century.

When Kate called or came by for a visit Brenda would busy herself with cleaning or straightening up, constantly talking about her schedule and what she had to do for the day. She knew Kate was not sympathetic to her about the situation she was now in, and she was only going to help her and give her advice about general housekeeping matters, keeping the girls' schedules on track to avoid too much interruption in their daily lives, and maybe provide her with some food or other necessities. It was understood that Brenda was not going to get to cry on Kate's shoulder and have her sit on the edge of the bed and stroke her head while Brenda poured out her heart about her disappointments. Kate was tough, and the lines of their relationship had always been clearly defined. Kate's view was that Brenda had made her bed, and now she would have to lay in it and tough it out. Brenda just went through the motions and wanted Kate to think she was doing the right things to hold her family together. The last thing Brenda wanted was for Kate to say, "I told you so." Even with knowing how Kate felt, it was still good to have her there, helping out with some of the chores, helping to take care of the girls, and somehow it made Brenda feel less alone, safe even.

When Kate wasn't around Brenda kept to her usual daily schedule. She woke the girls at 6am, went downstairs and put breakfast out for them to help themselves then go back upstairs to get 4-year-old Summer ready for daycare. Usually it was a box of cereal. On a good day when she had a little more time and energy, she would try her hand at a pot of Cream of Wheat, which she always made too lumpy and went to waste because the girls would eat around all of the lumps and throw the rest in the trash when she wasn't looking. But, on cereal days she would lay out four bowls and spoons for the girls. Other days, including weekends it was Swanson's breakfast T.V. dinners (frozen pancakes or dry scrambled eggs, each with one or two dry sausage links).

While Brenda got Summer ready, the other girls would be fighting for first shot at a hot shower in the bathroom. Usually it was nine-year-old

Sabrina who would win out, infuriating the other girls as they banged on the door, "Open the dooooor, I have to peeeee!" Sabrina would put her mouth to the crack in the door and taunt them, "You'll just have to wait. Go downstairs… or peeeee on yourself," then laugh and go back to brushing her teeth. By now Summer will have eaten a bowl of cereal, and gone into the living room to watch Bugs Bunny as she'd sit cross-legged on the thick-carpeted floor. Brenda would be in her room with the door closed, listening to all of the estrogen flying around her home. She looked over at the open closet door and saw her thick brown leather belt and sighed. She was hoping she wouldn't have to use it this morning. She was too tired and distracted to intercede today, so she let things play out.

Brenda rummaged through drawers looking for something comfortable to wear to walk the girls to school. She thought to herself 'No matter how much they fought, at least they had each other.' She didn't have the benefit as a child to grow up with her siblings, and she had always regretted that. All the girls loved each other, and really banded together once Jimmy left. But, as sisters do, they fought and argued over every little thing. Sabrina constantly reminded the other girls that she was the oldest, and when 'mommy wasn't around' SHE was in charge. Brenda was glad Sabrina was helping to keep the other girls in line, but it was also a bit of a challenge to keep her head from swelling out of the room about it when Brenda was around. Eight-year-old Cheresse was fairly quiet, but for the most part didn't take any mess from Sabrina. She would tell her big sister off if she tried to boss her around, "You can't tell me what to do. You are NOT my mother!" More often than the others Karla and Sabrina would fight all the time. Karla would get loud and threaten, "You better leave me alone, you ugly dog!" Sabrina would peek to make sure Brenda wasn't nearby and tauntingly muffle an overly animated laugh in her face, which would surely infuriate Karla.

Brenda refused to referee each and every disagreement in the house. She picked her battles to save her own sanity, and preferred to handle such situations with a hard, stern look at the instigator once they were in front of her. If it was an exceptionally terrible fight that slowed down the morning routine, or someone used particularly insulting or rude language toward the other, Brenda would simply jingle the buckle on her belt and each girl would freeze. The steel buckle hung heavily along one end and the thick brown leather strap carried 18 rows of three-holed perforations all along the back, and carried wind in the form of a whistle as it came down on the backside. It had a distinct sound when the thin cylinder tapped against the steel tip where the three metal prongs hung, and the girls could hear it from a great distance. Brenda knew how much power the belt had without even having to use it, and often used it successfully as an intimidation tool to regulate the house.

Brenda walked her daughters along the backstreets, up to Rockaway Boulevard, and across to the daycare at 145th Street, then cross over the Van Wyck Expressway to St. Clement's Pope Church School on 123rd Avenue. Mothers dropping off children would stop for a few minutes to chat and gossip about the high cost of living, child rearing, and politics, but also relationships. It seemed they were all waiting for Brenda to crack under the pressure of her life. Brenda didn't want to give them the satisfaction of seeing how shell-shocked and afraid she was. So, she kept the conversations brief.

The whole neighborhood had known about the fight she had with Jimmy years prior. But, Brenda avoided talking about it directly, and kept the conversation to the common, comfortable topics. She had been angry and embarrassed by the whole situation when it happened. Many of the other women weren't in better situations than she was, so she held her head high.

Dee Josephs was a lively light-skinned, full-busted woman with full lips, and large brown heavily mascaraed eyes, who lived a few blocks over from Brenda. She dyed her shoulder-length chestnut hair fire red two times per month partly because her sister was a beautician with her own salon, and partly because her husband loved red heads. When she flexed her hot temper, she would wear wigs in all different colors besides red just to spite him. She was a great listener, but an even bigger talker. She and her husband Earl had two sets of twins, Earl Jr. and Jared, and girls named Keely and Nelly. The girls were the same age as Sabrina, and her sons were five. Earl had a good paying job working as a foreman for a thriving local construction company. He made a decent amount of money to keep Dee comfortably at home with the kids. In return, Dee gave him hell and fought Earl like a wild cat. He would be in the shower getting ready for his night job, and she would leave the kids at home with him, take his car keys and drive Brenda to Green Acres shopping center so she could shop for groceries. He would be forced to phone a friend to pick him up and take him to work to make it on time. They would fight constantly. One fight ended with Dee smashing out his car windows with a bat and pouring a five-pound bag of sugar in Earl's gas tank. The Josephs had very public fist fights in the street over ridiculous things like how much Dee spent on school clothes for the girls, or Earl skipping out on a planned dinner with Dee's mother (who lived nearby and ran a home for foster children). She would beat him with kitchen utensils, furniture, and she even threw hot water on Earl as he ran for his life down the middle of their street wearing only his underwear. In spite of her wild ways, Brenda loved Dee because she always said what was on her mind, never held her tongue, and stood up for herself in any situation – all of the things Brenda had not yet learned how to do. Overall, Dee was a good mother, and Brenda learned a lot about how to juggle caring for multiple children. Eventually, Earl lost his job and couldn't pay the bills anymore. One day Earl woke up, got dressed to go out and look for a job, and never returned.

Moving On

Brenda was struggling to manage herself as well as her household. After the kids were off to school and she was home alone, most days Brenda would get back into bed, smoke her Salem 100's cigarettes and drink a can of beer or a glass of Scotch or Vodka with orange juice, whatever she had in the house. And she would do lots of crying, and sleeping. The reality was settling in that her four daughters now needed her in the same way she had needed her own biological mother, and she could not let them down. She wanted to blame it all on Jimmy. She felt blind-sided by his apparent disregard for her feelings and their friendship. She wanted to ask him, when did we stop being friends? It seemed like ages ago when they had stood up before Reverend Boyd in the middle of Kate and Dave's living room and said, "I do." She wasn't prepared then, and she certainly wasn't prepared for all of this.

She also hadn't planned to have so many children. But, Kate never educated her about birth control or even discussed what she should do as a married woman. And because Kate had kept her so sheltered, forging friendships and relationships with other women wasn't the most seamless of tasks. She didn't really have any other women she could sit down and speak with candidly about womanly issues, and about men. She felt a sadness that she didn't have her own birth mother to confide in or consult with about such things. Sure, Kate was, by all accounts, her mother. But, Brenda felt deep down inside that maybe if her birth mother knew what she was going through, she might want to offer support or advice or give her some hope. She reflected on Alice, and her relationship with Dill, and the painful reality was that Alice was also unprepared to handle her own husband, and her own marriage. She wondered which was better, a marriage with a man who mentally and physically abuses a woman, or a marriage that combusts and hurls the husband and the wife in opposite directions leaving nothing but toxic fallout. Either way, it wasn't a good situation.

> *A light sun shower was beginning to tap a tune on the window of Dr. Juwayriah's office. Brenda wondered if her cab would be on time for her pick-up, or would she have to wait outside in the rain without an umbrella. She was hardly prepared with cream linen pantsuit, tan leather Aerosoles sandals (her most comfortable pair), and a brown, leather waist pouch that fastened at the hip, where she carried her essentials, photo identification, cash, cherry-flavored Chap Stick, and her favorite, white peppermint TicTacs. Not that it mattered much.*

Cheresse had assured her the weather in Georgia was warm and sunny most of the year, and she was looking forward to that.

Brenda said, almost completely randomly, "You know, when you're a drug addict, there's never really one particular day when you start using drugs. When you're an addict all the days blend together, and life becomes one endless get high after another. It doesn't matter whether you have to get up to take the kids to school, or make breakfast, or do homework with the kids, or walk the dog. Everything gets pushed to the side, sometimes until the high comes down, or sometimes not even then."

Brenda prepared the girls for school and did her best to keep her house in order. But, at night, after everyone was asleep, she reflected on her life. She wondered what it would have been like if she had not become a mother, or hadn't gotten married. She wondered what her life would have been like if she had gotten that record deal and recorded and went on the road with the group. But, then she wouldn't have her beautiful girls, and she could not imagine her life without them. Then she'd curl up with a pillow, say a silent prayer to God asking for guidance, then fall off to sleep.

Elaine Cobb was an aide at Summer's school. She and Brenda were the same age, both single parents, and both loved music and dancing. On Fridays, Brenda would arrange for the girls to spend the night at Kate's, or she would ask Kate to stay with the girls at her house, so she could visit friends. Kate never asked who these new friends were, and Brenda did not offer any explanations. Truth was, Kate didn't mind babysitting her granddaughters on weekends as long as Brenda returned at a respectable hour. It gave Kate a chance to catch up with her grands, but also an opportunity to give Brenda's house a 'good deep cleaning,' which, in her opinion, was always overdue. She certainly didn't understand how years of her teaching Brenda that cleanliness was next to Godliness had been abandoned. But, then again, so many lessons she had raised Brenda on hadn't seemed to stick. She was spirited, even wayward. She certainly loved her daughter. Kate simply did not understand her choices over the past several years. In her mind, things really changed after Brenda met Jimmy, and she longed for the days when she was just a girl and things seemed so simple. "I could protect her back then," she thought. It pained her, thinking about her daughter struggling, and trying to feed her babies. But, Kate could not hold her up forever. "Galatians 6:5 For each will have to bear his own load." she thought to herself. And what she can't do, God will provide.

Brenda knew Kate would not stand for any late-night bar or nightclub hopping. So, she conveniently left that part out of her request for a sitter.

Leena

After a few short months, Elaine and Brenda had become inseparable. They went from very close friends to partners. Their daughters were in the same class, and they spent all of their free time together. It wasn't a committed, romantic relationship as much as it was companionship and support. They didn't make the nature of their relationship obvious for the sake of all the kids. So, after hours they would share their innermost thoughts and feelings, and tender moments through the night. Elaine would always make sure she was up and out of the house before Brenda's girls woke for school, and Brenda would do the same at Elaine's.

Bruer Bar was a neighborhood watering hole on Linden Boulevard where people in the Jamaica, Queens area loved to frequent. Everyone knew everyone else at Bruer Bar. It was a fun, safe, inexpensive place to have a drink, shoot pool, and listen to great music. It was not a rowdy establishment, and any riff raff that tried to start trouble would be quickly thrown out by the bouncer Ted "the Teddy Bear" Thomas. On the weekends when her kids were with Kate, Brenda could stay out, drink and dance until well past 3am. Elaine and Brenda would meet up with friends Josette (Jo), Frieda, and Elaine's best friend since chil .nood Leena.

Leena was 5 feet tall, with honey-brown skin, a close-cropped afro, button nose, almond eyes, and the prettiest white-toothed smile. She reminded Brenda of an adorable little cub. Her soft, shy speaking voice and tiny laugh was in sharp contrast to her powerful singing voice. To Leena, Brenda had a young spirit, a child-like innocence that she found rare and refreshing. They could talk for hours about silly things, agreeing that Chico Sticks were by far the best crunchy, peanut-buttery candy, Bugs Bunny was the king of cartoons, and Pam Grier was undoubtedly the foxiest babe on screen, hands down. Leena worked the day shift as a nurse at Queens Medical Center and was off on weekends. Without any children of her own to keep her at home, Leena could party all weekend. Brenda was envious of her independence, and greatly admired that Leena seemed to have her act together.

Frieda was a tall, thick, brown-skinned woman who wore square-rimmed pink eyeglasses, knee-length wrap skirts, and smoked a pack of cigarettes per day. Besides smoking, she was the good girl of the bunch. She was practical, level-headed, and more often than not served as the conscience of the group. Like Brenda, she had three daughters, and was on public assistance (but only briefly because she had been laid off from her job at the Queens Public Library). She didn't trust anyone, but her mother with her kids. So, if Mama couldn't babysit, she usually couldn't hang out.

Jo Moore was the social butterfly with no kids and an assortment of lovers who financed her party girl lifestyle. She was a free spirit with no interest in working a traditional job. On any given weekend she would appear, ready to party. She lived on Southern Fried Steak, collard greens, brandy, weed and lots of coke.

One evening, Leena, Brenda, Frieda and Jo were at The Champagne Grille off of Merrick Boulevard in Jamaica, NY, celebrating Leena's birthday. The club was owned by Leena's friend James, who had provided the ladies their third round of gin, and had finally coaxed her into getting up on stage to sing her favorite Big Maybelle songs. All three of them sitting on bar stools with their backs to the bar and facing the stage, boisterously cheering on their friend "Yeaah, Leena!!!" The first few bars of 'I Don't Want to Cry' spilled into the room, and Brenda was stunned.

Leena's husky, tortured voice leaned heavily on the notes of the saxophone, then spread across the rhythms of the piano, and settled softly with each stroke of the drum brush. The sadness and longing in the words, pleading for mercy, a failed love story seeming real to nearly every patron in the room by the expression on their faces. Brenda watched Leena, eyes closed, somewhere else, experiencing a love so deep, and a loss even deeper. Her voice filled the room in a surprisingly arresting way that had everyone mesmerized, unable to take their eyes off of Leena. This tiny version of Maybelle was belting out this big, rough, sad song, and Brenda couldn't take her eyes off of her. Brenda didn't realize she had been holding her breath until the song was over and everyone, including James, was applauding like crazy and stomping on the floor. Leena opened up her eyes and turned a little red from embarrassment, said thank you, and walked off stage and over to the bar. James handed her another gin with a huge smile on his face and said "See, I told you people wouldn't laugh. Girl, you got a gift!" Leena smiled nervously as she took a seat on the barstool next to Brenda, Frieda and Pam.

"Wow, that was amazing," Brenda said. Leena took a long gulp of the hot whiskey and paused. "What does it matter if you can't make no damn money off of it, right?" Leena said. It wasn't a question that she wanted answered, so Brenda didn't offer. Brenda could have shared her experience with being cheated out of her big chance at singing stardom, and her life being re-routed by marriage and children, but she didn't. She just sat silently and waited to see what else Leena was willing to share. Leena opened up, sharing that she started singing in her grandmother's choir when she was a girl. When she was 10 her uncle Thomas took her to see a record executive at TipToe Records in Shelton, New Jersey. He had heard they were looking for children to sing in commercials and variety television programs. But, they kept telling Uncle Thomas that her voice sounded too grown up. Her uncle had contacts in the music industry many years prior, but he had developed a gambling problem and a reputation for being a drunk. He stole money from family and friends over the years, so no one trusted him to conduct business on their behalf, except his sister June, Leena's mother. Despite her talent, Leena was unable to get her singing career off the ground. She eventually gave up her dream, and became a registered nurse at a local hospital. Singing was now something she only did in the shower (just like Brenda) until tonight.

The two were silent for a while. Occasionally someone would walk by and tell Leena how great she was and how she should 'do' something with her voice. She just smiled politely without saying anything in response. After the fourth or fifth person, she and Brenda looked at each other and started laughing so hard people began rolling their eyes and moving their seats. They couldn't stop laughing and had no idea why. They talked for a while longer and found comfort in the commonalities of their life experiences. The two friends had always hung out with the group, but never really talked to this degree. They had lots in common, from being divorced, spending part of their childhood growing up in Brooklyn, to their deep love of the same kinds of music. Brenda told her "A lot of people our age don't go around listening to Big Maybelle, you know?" Leena replied "Well, that's because they don't know nothin' 'bout GOOD music." They both fell out laughing.

Brenda began hanging out more and more with Leena, and was spending less time with Elaine. Elaine would ask her where she was going and where she had been, and Brenda would make excuses or not answer. For the first time, she felt she had a real connection with someone. A friend who really understood her, and quite frankly she thought she deserved it. She had always put everyone else's feelings ahead of her own, and she was tired of it. Being in Leena's company was like breathing fresh air, almost seductive, and she wanted that feeling all the time.

After one evening of too many drinks, and too many joints, Leena's eyes popped opened to find herself curled up in Brenda's bed, naked and wrapped in Brenda's sleepy, warm embrace. She didn't jump up right away, or say a word. She lay there for a few minutes, half enjoying the comfort of it all, but mostly trying to figure out how she had gotten there and what this all meant. Of course, Leena knew Brenda was gay, and that she and her best friend had a thing going on. She even knew Brenda was attracted to her. But, she honestly had never thought of herself as gay. Was she gay, too? Did this officially make her gay? What did she actually DO last night? Will Brenda think they were girlfriends now? 'Won't it be pretty awkward when we get up?' she thought. Does this mean we won't be able to be friends or hang out anymore? So many questions were swirling. Leena certainly didn't see herself living the life of a gay woman. She liked men too much for that, right? She also didn't think she wanted to be with men AND women. It seemed very complicated, and she didn't want to deal with it all right now. She liked her simple life the way it was. 'How am I supposed to look my best friend in the eye?' she panicked. No, NO, she had to stop this thing right now. It wouldn't be fair to keep it going.

She wriggled out of Brenda's grip, reached down on the floor to get her dress, and stood up. She pulled it over her head and shook Brenda awake. When Brenda opened her eyes, she saw Leena standing there and smiled. Then she noticed Leena's face was not smiling back, and hers turned to concern. "What's wrong, what happened?" Brenda said looking around the room. Leena blurted it out "We can't hang out anymore." She hadn't thought it out completely, and immediately felt confusion and desperation. The urgency of it felt very necessary then, and she couldn't take the time to figure it out right now. She knew she had to go, and she knew she couldn't just leave without ending it. Brenda was pained by the fear in her friend's face, and didn't say anything further. There was really nothing left to say. She watched as Leena turned, walked out of her bedroom and closed the door behind her.

Brenda curled her knees to her chest, pulled the covers up to her neck, and then sobbed heavily into her pillow like a baby. The pain was unbearable. Her stomach felt empty and hot and queasy, and she felt like she couldn't breathe. She didn't know if it was from last night's drinking or the pain of doing something that drove her only real friend away. She tried to recall every conversation, every laugh, every moment from the previous night. She thought she had read a connection between her and Leena. It all seemed so mutual, and consensual to her. Did she misread Leena's cues??? No, she couldn't have. She didn't force Leena to do anything. She was always clear about who she was, and what she was looking for... wasn't she? Then she thought about how Leena WAS Elaine's best friend, and how wrong she was cutting Elaine short to hang with Leena. And that's when karma reached around and took a big bite on the right cheek of her foul behind. And she knew she deserved this. It had served her right. It was wrong. She HAD secretly been lusting after her girlfriend's best friend under the guise of friendship. But, if she were really being honest with herself, she was confusing lust with friendship. One can never really have both, not really. She wanted Leena's friendship more than anything, even more than the intimacy. She wanted her to be the sister she could talk to, and laugh with, and sit around listening to old music with. Why did she have to go and ruin everything??!! Damnit! What was she going to do now? She had to apologize. She had to tell Leena they could just be friends, nothing more.

She called Leena numerous times for weeks to try salvaging their friendship, but Leena did not return any of her calls. After a month, Brenda went by Leena's apartment, and found her apartment completely empty. Her landlord told Brenda that Leena had secured a nursing job upstate New York and moved the previous week. Brenda wondered if Elaine knew about what had gone on that night, but wasn't letting on. Too embarrassed and afraid to bring Leena up to Elaine, she never brought Leena up again... and neither did Elaine.

New Beginnings

By summer, Brenda and Elaine were back to where they were in the beginning of their relationship, lovers and good friends. They were partying more than ever, drinking and getting high every weekend. Frieda asked them to be her guest at an exclusive, invitation-only party at the J25 Club, a loft warehouse on the lower west side of Manhattan.

Frieda's friend Mary told her about these special Friday night parties that were different from any parties she had been to before, and they were lots of fun. Mary worked at Apple Bank as a Branch Manager during the day. But, at night she loved to party in Manhattan. Brenda and Elaine got dressed up and went to check it out. Kate had already picked up the girls for the weekend. She packed their bags, kissed and hugged each of them, and told them she'd see them on Sunday. "Have fun with your Nana, and tell Pop-Pop I said hi, ok?" Brenda planned to enjoy the peace and quiet of the house with Elaine, and hang out all the way until Sunday! She bought a white, flare-legged pantsuit and a pair of green platform shoes. The suit wasn't tight, but it accentuated her round hips and curves in all the right places, and she knew it. She wore the white, button-down vest over a solid green, silk long-sleeved shirt. She picked her afro out, looked in the mirror, and knew she looked sharp. Elaine wore a suede patchwork red, rust, brown and gold mini skirt with a matching vest that laced up her flat belly with suede straps, and tall, red patent leather boots that zipped up to the knee. The top pushed her boobs up and close to her chest, and made her look very busty. Brenda thought she looked super-hot. They met Mary at her place in Brooklyn, smoked a couple of joints, and they headed out to The J. Mary wore a red and black floral print wrap-around dress with black platform shoes. Men loved Mary's shape: 32B bust, 26 waist, 40 hips. So, her dresses were usually loose on top, but tight around the butt and thigh area. She wore a long blonde wig with loose, flowing curls.

Mary hung out often and knew all of the club managers and bouncers. She also knew most of the guys who funded parties like the ones at The J, which required lots of cash. Brenda couldn't wait to see what The J was all about.

It was very crowded outside the club, with the line to enter wrapping around the corner. People were dressed in all different ranges of outfits from shiny pants, leopard fur jackets, big hats with feathers sticking out on one side, big afros, colorful shirts unbuttoned down to the chest hairs, long flowing skirts, and plenty of glitter make up. Brenda was excited. Everyone looked good, including her. This wasn't the Bruer Bar crowd, that's for sure. Mary waved to a white guy at the door named Nate, who let them walk ahead of the line and into the party. Brenda noticed Mary had slipped a small bag of something into Nate's hand as she hugged him on the way in. She didn't ask any questions.

From the outside of The J they could only feel the heavy bass vibration of the music inside, but no specific song could be identified from where they were standing. It was only when they walked through the entryway could they make out the music and hear the words, feel the vibration move through their bodies, and smell the sweat, alcohol, money and drugs. Brenda could barely breathe. 'Love Rollercoaster' by the Ohio Players was playing and she immediately felt the heartbeat of the club. Some people were standing at the bar, drinking and talking. Others were gathered around long, low tables with white powder spread across the entire length of the tabletop. People were bending down on either side snorting fresh cocaine through straws that sat in tall silver metal cups in the middle of the tables. Guests were not required to pay for the cocaine. It was there for anyone who wanted it. The idea was to get you to try it and then you went to see 'a man' at the back of the club for more if you wanted to buy. The drinks were not free, but they were discounted if you were a 'member'. Brenda had never tried cocaine before, but she wasn't against seeing what all the talk was about. They mingled for a bit by the bar, and then Mary took her around to meet some of her friends.

Mary spotted her friend Pam sitting at a V.I.P. table with 3 well-dressed men and one woman. Pam was bent over the table with her bronze, cleavage-revealing top, and gold glittered miniskirt. This woman oozed sex appeal. She was extremely thin and stood about 5'7". She had a pretty, bright white smile that could be seen from across the room, a slight gap between her two front teeth. When she smiled her eyes disappeared under her eyelids making her look cat-like, but when she wasn't smiling you could see how big and pretty her hazel eyes were. She wore her natural hair in a curly-afro style that she liked to brush back or to one side. Her favorite drink was Jack Daniels and Coke, and she absolutely loved to sniff cocaine. As Billy Paul belted out 'Meeee aaaand Mrs., Mrs. Joooones, Mrs. Jones, Mrs. Jones, Mrs. Joooones…' Brenda thought she had just seen an Angel on earth.

Brenda was enjoying her freedom from Jimmy, and some financial independence from Kate and Dave. After weeks of neglecting their responsibilities, Brenda and Elaine called it quits. They decided it was time to focus on raising their kids and getting their lives in order. They had been going out with Mary and meeting up with Pam, who had endless access to weed, alcohol, and coke. By now, Brenda had gotten a real taste for it, and it was good. But it was a habit she simply could not afford.

Brenda had wrongly assumed public assistance was paying her utility bills, which she never inquired about after Jimmy left. So, when she received a whopping $19,000 electric bill, she nearly fell apart. She was warned that if she failed to pay the bill, she would lose her housing stipend. Using only her warm personality, she was able to secure a waitress job at the new Howard Johnson hotel near JFK airport in its restaurant to help bring in some extra cash and keep her home. Unfortunately, she was unable to manage it all. So, she contacted the NYC Housing Authority to let them know she couldn't keep up the payments on her house, and requested additional assistance in finding an apartment for her family. It took two years for Housing to contact Brenda about an available apartment in a fairly new complex in Brooklyn, called Linden Plaza Apartments.

She went to check out the apartment. When she got off the B17 bus on Linden Boulevard in East New York, she looked up to see a monstrous complex raised four stories off of the ground, with two massive buildings escaping into the clouds. To enter the complex, she had to either walk up a long zig-zag staircase between the two buildings, or she could walk up one of two very long ramps that spanned the length of both buildings and meet in the center at the top close to where the stairs ended. She wanted to see how it would feel to climb the ramp, so she took that route. She was thinking how fun, and how dangerous, it would be if the girls rode on their bikes, or skates down the long ramp. She made a mental note to ban them from doing so right away.

Slightly winded but not out of breath, she reached the top and her breath was taken away by what she saw. Hidden from the street was a beautiful, wide-open community of five buildings (not two), and an arrangement of two-family town houses in front of each tall building. It was as if each building had its own neighborhood, but all five communities were one organism. Throughout the complex were well-maintained, manicured trees and short green bushes, each potted and surrounded in 10-foot by 10-foot red, brick square structures with beige borders. These structures were neatly arranged around the building like broccoli squares to complement the main course. She turned her head toward the sky to see the massive 17-story building wrapped in terraces, seemingly one for each apartment. The one she was there to see was located on the 10th floor. Immediately, she worried about Summer's safety. She made another mental note to shake the metal slats when she got upstairs. She went around to the front of the building and entered the community of 'building 1', her destination. She saw how alive the place was. She walked the long, outside corridor to get to the entrance of the building. There were small children playing a game of tag, teenage boys using the side of the building to play a game of handball, a few adults seated on two benches built into the frame of one of the broccoli squares. They were watching three girls playing a game of double-dutch across from the entrance. People took note of her, but quickly went back to what they were doing. She entered the glass doors to the building and was buzzed in by the security officer posted in the lobby. She liked the idea of security and a posted guard. She announced to the guard she was there to see an apartment. He asked her to wait there while he called the management office. There were no chairs in the lobby, so she stood and waited. The lobby smelled of something soft and sweet. She looked around and spied a little room across the lobby that housed the mailboxes for each apartment. She looked down the long hallway and saw five brown doors, the closest of which was open, with a bright yellow light that spilled out onto the hallway floor. She recognized the scent of fabric softener, the low hum of clothes dryers and chatter. Laundry room. The guard called her over and handed her a key. He instructed her to take one of the three elevators up to the 10th floor, make a left and go all the

way to the end of the hallway to the E apartment on the left. "Good luck"

he smiled, then returned to his post. Brenda smiled back and said "Thank

you." She turned to three elevators, pressed the 'up' button, and the

center elevator doors opened. Traveling up, alone in that elevator, she

was excited, nervous, and hopeful about what she would see upstairs.

She looked at the key in her hand. If this was the right one, it would be

her very first apartment on her own, with no help from Jimmy, or Dave

or Kate. She took a deep breath. When the elevator door opened, she

stepped out onto a deserted hallway. It had butter yellow, textured

wallpapered walls, separated by long rows of brown doors on either side

of the elevator bank. She passed apartment doors that on her left, started

with 'A' and across from that was apartment 'L'. So, the other side of

the elevator bank must be the remainder of the alphabet. There was a

skinny brown door with a sign that read 'Compactor Room'. She turned

the doorknob and saw a little room no bigger than a closet with a handle

on the wall meant to open the chute so that trash bags could be shoved

inside. She closed the door and continued down the hall, passing

apartments B, C and D until she reached the end. On the left was 'E' and

on the right was 'F'. She liked that it was in the corner. That meant the windows in the apartment would be facing in two directions. She was excited to see the view.

As soon as she walked into the apartment, she knew she wanted it. It had a full kitchen she could enter from either side (one side close to the front door, the other opened out onto the dining room). There were three spacious bedrooms, one full and one-half bath, and lots of closets. The living room was bright, and received lots of natural light from the terrace that ran the length of the apartment. So, the dining room, living room, and two of the bedrooms all had a beautiful view of sky and community. She opened the glass doors and stepped out onto the terrace, closed her eyes and took a deep breath. She looked out at the panoramic view from left to right. She loved that the view was facing the back of the building, where there were no handball games and no double-dutch being played, just the quiet breeze elevated into the clouds. It was just a quiet view of Queens, a place where she had come from. This place would represent the future. She reached down and grabbed the railing, shaking it in several places, especially at each end, making sure it was safe. She was home.

Unraveling

Kate and Dave came to see the new apartment and visit with the girls one day. They sat Brenda down and told her she needed to start being a mother to her children. She couldn't really argue the point. She knew it was true. She was feeling tired all the time, and nearly missed one of the girls' dance recitals after doing drugs all night. She had already failed at marriage, but her girls were the four things she didn't want to fail at.

She didn't completely stop hanging out with her friends, just slowed her partying all the way down to approximately once per month. The best part of hanging out with Elaine, Mary and Pam was, of course, Pam. Brenda made it a point to keep in contact with Pam, calling her every few months, just to see how she was doing. Pam always greeted her with "Hey, Baby," which released butterflies in her stomach, and made her feel like a girl again. Pam was so sexy, carefree, and exciting. Brenda often had fantasies about her and Pam being a couple.

Pam had visited Brenda a few times in Brooklyn, and every so often they would smoke a little weed, drink, listen to music and laugh a lot.

Brenda genuinely loved Pam's company. She was easy to talk to, and was a great listener. She knew Brenda was on public assistance, and sometimes gave her a couple of hundred dollars to buy food for her and the girls between welfare checks.

Pam didn't want any children of her own, but she loved Brenda's girls. They called her Aunt Pam, and she seemed to really like them. She enjoyed watching Brenda being a mom. She thought it was cute and admired that Brenda was brave enough to be responsible for four other lives. "I'm too selfish" she'd tell Brenda. She thought of her own mother, a homemaker always struggling to feed her and her two siblings. She didn't want to struggle that way. She liked being able to get up and go. It worked for her. Pam's visits were always brief, only staying for a few hours. Then she, her fur stoles, bare-backed dresses, and high heels would be out the door and off to some party. Sadly, Brenda knew she would never be able to tie Pam down.

For the most part, things had become civil between Brenda and Jimmy. Not loving, or overly-friendly the way they used to be, but at least civil, 'for the girls' sake.' Jimmy had seemingly moved on and was making a life for himself with a stable job, an apartment, and, from what Brenda could make out from his phone conversations with their daughters, he was seriously dating someone. She was only slightly jealous. She had always wanted the best for him and his life, and she hoped he would find love. She thought about how they used to harmonize together to some of the most beautiful love songs. It took them to a world of storybook love, connected hearts, and passion. Love songs of the 40's and 50's were tasteful classics that were timeless. They both had an understanding and an appreciation for the lyrics, the melodies, the harmonies, the instruments, and the arrangements. To Brenda, it felt like such a long time ago. She hoped he was happy. She also wanted to find a piece of happiness for herself.

Brenda was more determined than ever to enjoy her life. She and the girls had settled into their new apartment, and the kids made friends quickly. But, Brenda was getting restless. She didn't see herself merely sitting home cooking and cleaning. She also didn't want to just sit outside on the bench with the other single mothers in the building. She wanted to dress up, go out, party, and forget about everything the way she did in Queens. It was fun, and she missed it. She also missed her partying friends. She even missed the drugs. Everything seemed so much easier when she was high. She could see the judgmental eyes of Kate and Dave, telling her how to raise the girls, criticizing her choices in friends and being all judgey. She could hear them scolding her like she was a child, and she became defiant in her mind. She was grown now! They couldn't tell her what to do. She was taking care of her kids now, even if it was with the help of welfare. She was taking care of things on her own. This made her feel empowered. At the same time, she didn't want to lose sight of what was most important, and that was her daughters. She just had to find some balance, she thought.

She was smoking lots of weed on a regular basis, started drinking more and resumed hanging out with her friends, sometimes all night long. Hearing the water running in the shower close to bedtime became a familiar sound for the girls. It meant that 'Mommy was going out for the night'. As Brenda walked from the bathroom to her bedroom in a large yellow bath towel, Cheresse followed her and asked "Ma, you going out?" She wanted to add "again" but thought better of it. Brenda unabashedly dropped her towel on the bed and began slathering fragrant lotion all over. Annoyed at the imposition, Cheresse looked away from her mother and instead peered out the bedroom window, and at the glowing lights over Queens. Brenda replied distractedly, "Mmhmm" as she rubbed musk oil on her hands and smeared it across the tops of her breasts, underneath them and down to areas she taught Cheresse were private. 'Obviously this did not apply' to Brenda, thought Cheresse. She was behaving very differently, and Cheresse and her sisters all noticed the change in their mother. "Make sure the other girls eat and go to bed soon. You know Karla does not like to get up in the morning for school." Cheresse glared at her mother's back as she slipped a tan blazer over a white silk shirt and wide-legged brown slacks and boots. "What am I supposed to feed them? There's no food in the house!" Cheresse said a little too panicked, and a little too loud. Brenda paused, looked over her shoulder at her daughter, gave her a frustrated sigh, and made her way to the kitchen. Cheresse followed. Brenda opened the refrigerator. Cheresse was right, there really was NO food in the fridge. A half-empty jar of sweet pickles, an empty bottle of Catsup, a stick of margarine, a pitcher with one swallow of grape Kool Aid, four slices of Wonder Bread (two of the slices were ends), and two soft, rotting onions. "Shit" she whispered under her breath. She hadn't meant to wait so long to get groceries. The time had gotten away from her somehow. Not that she had the money to go 'big' food shopping anyway. She reached into her pocket and handed Cheresse $5. "Run to the store and get a loaf of bread. At least y'all can have peanut butter and jelly tonight. Cheresse looked at the $5 bill in her hand, then back at her mother. It was 9:30 p.m. Did she really expect her to put her street clothes back on and go all the way to the Sutter Avenue bodega for bread...ALONE?? Brenda opened the cabinet and grabbed the peanut butter, slamming it down onto the counter. A mama cockroach and her baby scurried behind the stove out of sight. "I'll be back" Brenda announced before walking out the door. Cheresse stood there for a moment, confused and hot with anger, not understanding how her mother expected her to go out to the store at that time of night to get bread. She changed her clothes, grabbed her jacket and went to the store. When she returned, she made sandwiches for her sisters and poured them cups of water. They all ate their sandwiches in silence and went to bed. When the alarm clock woke them up in the morning, the younger girls fought for space at the bathroom sink to brush their teeth, while Cheresse peeked into her mother's bedroom. The bed was still made up, and the room was empty. She closed the door and went to dress for school.

Jimmy would come to the apartment complex to pick up the girls on special occasions, but would meet them downstairs where he parked on the street. He would take them to a dude ranch, or to a state park for a picnic. He would also take them out after an annual dance production, or celebrate their birthdays. He never missed a graduation or any other major event in their lives, but day-to-day it felt like they were fatherless like their friends.

On one such visit, Sabrina and Cheresse confided in their Dad that Brenda was hanging out late, sometimes not coming home, and she was occasionally having strange women sleeping over. Cheresse had even caught Brenda and a woman having sex. This infuriated Jimmy beyond measure. He remembered how he felt when he had caught Brenda's friends naked all over his living room floor in their Queens home. He couldn't imagine how his young, confused daughters must be feeling, and he died a little more inside at the thought. He knew they couldn't speak up, but he could. He had to! After the girls kissed their Dad, and went inside of the building, Jimmy asked "Can we talk for a minute?" Brenda looked incredulous already. She had her arms folded and was puffing on a cigarette. She was still a little high from the joint she smoked 30 minutes prior, and Jimmy was messing with her high. "What do you want to talk about?" she asked blowing out smoke a little too close to Jimmy's non-smoker's nose. He didn't know how to broach such an awkward subject, but he was too furious to care. He threatened her saying "I won't stand by and watch you put my daughters in danger." "What the hell are you talking about DANGER?! I would never hurt my girls!!" He told her what his daughters said, and although her first response was embarrassment, it quickly turned to indignance. Brenda snapped "You can't tell me what to do with my life, Jimmy!" She paused,

sighing "You never could handle all of this" waving her hand around the

room and landed it on her right hip. "My kids are *not* in any danger!

Just mind your own damn business" she said. "My kids ARE my

BUSINESS!" he shot back. Brenda squinted her eyes and leaned in,

letting him know she was not backing down. And in a voice seething

with resentment, she whispered "They weren't your business when you

walked out the door…" She let that hang in the air. And as she watched

the pain, hurt and sadness wash over his soft, watery eyes, she felt bad

for him. She knew full well that it cut him deeply. But, she couldn't

take it back now. She threw her cigarette butt down near his shoe, then

turned her back and went upstairs to 'her' apartment. After that, Jimmy

instructed the girls to meet him downstairs so that he wouldn't have to

see or fight with Brenda in front of their children.

Jimmy called and told Brenda he was getting married. He said he

wanted to tell Sabrina and Cheresse in person, and made plans to pick

them up for a visit. He explained that Karla and Summer were not old

enough to understand, and that he would tell them later. When he met

with his two eldest daughters and announced he was getting married they

didn't have much reaction. They didn't know how to feel. They

understood that their parents were not getting back together, but they didn't understand why he was announcing his new marriage to them so formally. He seemed happy, so they were happy for him. They wondered who this new woman was in their dad's life, and how she would fit into their father-daughter visits. Jimmy explained that her name was Sophia Riveiro and he loved her very much. He said she was a nice woman who treated him well, and made him happy. That was it. He told them they were going to be flower girls in the wedding, and that he would make all the arrangements for them to be there. He did just that. Jimmy and Sophia married on July 28, 1974, with Jimmy's two eldest daughters walking down the aisle as flower girls in polyester pink dresses, pink floral headbands stuck in their wide afros, and white patent leather shoes on their feet. It was a joyous day in Jimmy's life, surrounded by Sophia's family, their friends, and Reggie as best man. He had finally found a sweet, normal piece of happiness for himself.

Ida Mae

Jaywayriah: In the past, you've spoken about your time with Mae as the most damaging of your life. You've been through lots of other things that could appear much more affecting. Why do you think you had such a hard time pulling yourself and your children out of it? Do you feel as if you always had the power?

Brenda: No, no I didn't have the power. I wasn't prepared for someone like Mae. She was more dangerous than anyone I've ever met in my life Doc. And, I've met some dangerous people. Mae was the Devil.

Ida Mae used her behind to push open the heavy brown wooden doors of Sugar's Bar & Lounge. The familiar scent of freshly consumed liquor, cigarette smoke and sweat rushed past her out the door and into the rain. She peeked over her right shoulder discretely conducting a two-second scan of the room to be sure it was safe to go inside. She shook off the long, black Louis Vuitton umbrella and fastened the snap to keep it from wetting her shoes and bags. She looked over her other shoulder to be sure no one was following her, and entered with the assured confidence she was known for.

She was born Ida Mae Fuller, but everyone called her 'Broadway Mae'. Silky, her pimp, branded her with it because she had made a name for herself as the preferred flavor of black and white men from NYC to Hollywood. She was 4' 11", light-skinned with a small-waisted, and with very large breasts. Her breasts were her biggest assets. She had slightly slanted eyes accentuated by thinly penciled in eyebrows and long false eyelashes. Her lady mustache teetered on sexy, and could become unruly if neglected for more than a day or two. On the left side of her face and slightly above her top lip was a tattooed on black mole she thought made her look sensual.

As a child she was called Hollywood Mae by the owner of a local television station in Sheltsburg, South Carolina in 1955 when she was just 5 years old.

Ida Mae was a local performer who sang gospel songs every Sunday morning on Channel 3 – KGOD. She was 'the darling' the Carolinians waited to see on the show, with her fair skin, long, wavy black hair that her mother and manager, Prentice Smiley, paid to have done up in spiral pin curls every Saturday, and her golden, big-girl voice. If you turned away from the television you would have thought Ms. Mahalia Jackson was singing. Her voice wasn't as deep as Ms. Mahalia's, but she came pretty close to the real thing. And Prentice knew it. So, she piled Ida Mae's hair high up on her head and pinned it up tight, just the way Mahalia would wear hers. And she would dress her in very modest yellow, pink or lavender dresses with embroidery that wasn't too flashy, but subtly appealing to the studio audience's eyes for a Sunday morning. When Ida Mae would sing 'Go Tell It On The Mountain' (1950), the phones in the station would ring with compliments about Ida Mae's voice.

Mae walked over to the bar, gently placed her oversized signature brown Louis Vuitton satchel on the empty stool next to her, and three large, overstuffed shopping bags onto the floor. She peeled back the wet hood of her fitted black rain slicker so that the rainwater hit the floor behind her chair instead of on her outfit. Unzipping her bag, she casually pulled out a delicate red leather cigarette case and removed a single Virginia Slims cigarette, firmly positioning it on the left side of her thin, shiny red lips. She placed her elbows on the bar, and leaned forward slightly staring impatiently at Yvette the bartender. Yvette scrambled to grab the lighter from under the bar and lit Mae's cigarette. Mae took a long drag then moved the cigarette away from her mouth, blew smoke up toward the ceiling and watched it fold over onto itself, slow-grinding with the existing smoke and music that hovered over the bar like an old faithful lover. She swiveled her bar stool around so she could survey the room, and took inventory of the patrons, many of whom she had seen before. Smitty, one of the neighborhood 'numbers' men, was sitting at a small cocktail table on the far wall fully engaged in his own important conversation, as usual. Mae had seen the woman sitting across from him before, but she didn't know her. She took inventory of the woman from head to toe before she turned her attention back toward the door.

It was 4:30 p.m. and the bar was half filled with regulars. The husky, thick voice of Tina Turner wailed loudly behind the fast guitar licks and frantic horn section, filling the dimly lit room. Mae slid her thick 4 foot 10 inch frame off the stool causing her raincoat to fall down off her shoulders and drape backwards over the stool legs. She wore a shimmering silver painted-on cat suit that zipped all the way up the front of her body from the center of her vagina to the top of her rib cage. The top of the zipper struggled to contain her full breasts which were visible and being admired by everyone in the room, including Brenda. The suit showed off every curve of her body and she loved it. The 5-inch heel of her black patent leather pumps helped elongate her tiny frame. Her long, curly black wig flowed past her shoulders and halfway down her back. Ordinarily, this would have pleased her and she would have sashayed slowly past all the patrons so they could get a good look. But, tonight she needed to cautiously pace herself. Spotting a small, empty table in the back of the bar, she walked toward it at a cool, steady pace, smiling and giving a 'hey' to Ann the waitress and others she knew. She unloaded the heavy satchel onto a chair and pulled it up real close to her, then sat down. The bar patrons went back to their usual conversations and laughter, and this suited Ida Mae just fine. She needed to stay out of plain sight tonight. She had been in hiding for two weeks, and she needed to get back to the apartment to swap out some clothes and store some things. "Hey, Vette" she said. "What time is Barbara coming in tonight?" "She's working the 11 to 7 shift," said Yvette. Mae looked at her Patek Philippe bracelet watch and noted she had some time to kill. She had been laying low at her good friend Barbara's apartment for the first couple of weeks after her release. But, she had to travel to Boston, Connecticut and North Jersey to establish some connections. She was now back and, having left her key at the apartment, she needed to wait for Barbara to gain access. Yvette reached behind the bar for a sealed white envelope and handed it to Mae "But she left this for you." Mae took the envelope and opened it. Inside was a single key to Barbara's apartment, and a simple note. 'Mae, Silky's got a handle on you. Whatever you're gonna do, make it quick. Be safe." No signature. She looked around the bar, but her face did not show the sheer panic she felt in her belly. She had to play it cool, and think what to do next. She needed a drink.

Eleven years earlier, Mae had risen to become Silky's main score. She had made more money for him in one year than all of his whores combined since he became a pimp. She was hot, knew how to rake a john's pockets, and was a sharp, professional businesswoman. He loved having her by his side, because she made him look good. He trusted her to keep the other whores in line as well, something he felt he shouldn't have to waste his valuable time doing. She looked soft and frilly with all her leopard and feathers and sexy-girl persona. But, deep down inside she was a wild, strong country bobcat who could wrestle a 200 lb. man to the ground and win. She was cunning and Ida Mae was fully aware of her value and reminded Silky about it on numerous occasions up until the time Sarah had arrived. So, imagine Mae's surprise when Silky announced to the entire 'family' that Sarah would be his new main whore.

Sarah was a shapely, blond girl with a pretty face, originally from Minnesota. Silky had brought her back to New York from California a month before. He immediately began showing her off around town and introducing her to key players in the game, which raised Ida Mae's eyebrow, but she really wasn't threatened at first because she knew her position. Mae was confident Sarah had nothing on her, until Silky 'brought her out.' Mae did not take kindly to being bumped down to second place, or to being edged out of her top clients. They tipped her well, on the side, and she wasn't about to lose out on all that cash.

On a cold November day, Silky gathered his team of whores to his office on Jamaica Avenue and 167th Street. It was an office space located on the 5th floor of a building with a dry- cleaning business on the ground floor. Silky's associate, Big Joe ran the cleaners for a Korean couple who enjoyed collecting a monthly fee and didn't ask questions. Sixteen whores, including Mae, plus Silky's right hand man, Lucky, Sarah and Silky assembled. Bottles of champagne were chilling in ice buckets around the office. All the girls speculated about what the announcement was, and wondered whether or not there was more money to be made once announced. Silky called everyone to attention and was about to place Sarah in the middle of the room to address everyone, the same way he had done for Mae six years prior. Mae didn't give Silky or Sarah a chance to speak. She pulled out the machete she always kept hidden in her huge satchel and lunged at Sarah's throat, missing her jugular by 1/8th of an inch. All the girls scattered from the office. Silky sent Lucky to take care of the girls. He was left with the two women fighting. Sarah screamed and tried to run behind Silky, but she tripped on the leg of Silky's black metal desk, and fell to the floor. "Shit" Silky shouted. "I aint getting' my new suit dirty wit you crazy bitches tonight!" Mae pulled her .38 from her bag and aimed it at Sarah, but Sarah jumped toward Mae catching and forcing her right hand down, causing a round to go off. Silky screamed "What the FUCK?!' as he fell back in his chair, his wide brimmed hat dropped back onto the floor. The bullet hit Mae in the left calf. "Mother Fucker!!!" Mae screamed in pain. Now she was really pissed. With blood trailing down the side of her leg, Mae reached out and caught a tight hold around Sarah's neck and squeezed hard. Silky tried to get close to break them up, but the gun and the machete were both flailing wildly, and he couldn't get close. Part of him was turned on by all the entangled 'tits and ass', but he knew he had to break it up because this was messing up his money. Sarah tried to crawl out of Mae's grasp, but Mae grabbed Sarah by her right leg and used the machete to slice her from the back of the knee down to the back of her ankle, like the seam of a stocking. "AHHHHHH! YOU CRAZY BITCH!!!" Sarah screamed, trying to pull her leg away from Mae. Blood shot out onto the wall and all over the carpet. "SHIT!" Silky said as he launched forward and grabbed Sarah dragging her out of the office into the hallway away from Mae.

Mae had turned to check the gunshot in her leg, grabbed a cloth napkin from the floor and tied off the gunshot to slow the bleeding. Then she pulled herself up to a standing position using the desk, and made her way out into the hallway after Silky and Sarah, with her .38 still in her hand. Silky knew Ida Mae was crazy enough to kill Sarah, so he dragged Sarah into elevator and pressed the 'G' button frantically. Sarah lay on the elevator floor bleeding and screaming in pain. "We gonna get you all fixed up, Baby, don't you worry. Hang in there." Seeing the elevator doors closing, Silky slid down to the floor of the elevator and pulled Sarah up leaning her back onto his chest. Sarah was hysterically crying now, inconsolable. She was bleeding all over his new blue suit, and he was pissed about it. Silky was already vowing to take all of the medical expenses and his dry-cleaning bill out of Mae's pay. He would deal with her later, he thought. But, before the doors could close Ida Mae caught the door with her good leg, and pushed it open. She reached in with her .38, then fired off three shots, one hitting Silky in the left foot, and the other two landed where she had intended, one in Sarah's chest and the other in the center of Sarah's forehead.

Fast-forward, three years after Mae was sentenced to seven years for killing Sarah, and shooting Silky, she was released early for good behavior (thanks to a special arrangement she had made with the warden). Her only request was a quiet release so that Silky would have no idea she was getting out. This would buy her some time to get things set up, make enough money and get lost so he could never find her and retaliate.

She had always stashed away emergency money, and with Silky looking for her, she knew she could be dead if she didn't take that money to get away and hide quickly. She needed to find a place where Silky would never think to look for her.

Yvette turned down a cocktail napkin and asked, "What can I get for ya, Ida Mae?" "A Chivas straight, baby, thanks", said Mae. Ann responded, "You got it" and off she went. Ida Mae rummaged through her bag, taking a quick inventory of what she had hurriedly thrown in. She was most concerned with her stack of cash and her big black address book. Everything else was secondary. She had left her most cherished items at Barbara's (pictures of her 10-year-old son Neville, pictures of grandma Jesse, Mae's original birth certificate (not the two fakes she had in her satchel), and a $20,000.00 cashiers' check made out to herself). She knew they would be safe with Barbara. She knew Barbara from prison, and she could certainly handle herself with Silky or any other man. By the time the full inventory had been taken her drink arrived. She leaned back and took a long, quiet sip, and let her brain work out a plan to get herself out of this situation.

That familiar faced woman caught her eye again. Her wheels started to turn. Mae crossed her legs and locked in a stare that she had used many times before. The woman was attractive, wide-hipped like Mae, and appeared slightly drunk already. Mae noted it was only 7 PM. The woman was only half chatting with Bennett, a man Ida Mae knew from when she first came to New York. When she saw Bennett catch a glimpse of her, she motioned for him to come over to her. He excused himself and went over to Ida Mae. With his mouthwatering and half smacking, he said, "Hey, Ida Mae. What's good tonight?" Ida Mae replied, "Heyyy there, Ben. You lookin' kinda fine tonight. You all dressed up for your date over there?" "Nah", Ben replied. "That's my girl Brenda. She just stopped in for a drink on her way home." He paused, "You wanna meet her?" Ben already knew Mae wanted to meet Brenda, but he was playing coy. "Sure, bring her on over, Ben. Y'all sit on down let me buy you a drink."

Mae noticed Brenda was friendly, but seemed somewhat distant, shy even. Ben carried the conversation for the better part of twenty minutes, while Ida Mae stared through Brenda, and Brenda focused on the permanent cigarette burn on Mae's side of the table, which was, at that moment, positioned directly under Ida Mae's very revealing cleavage.

Ben excused himself since his job was done, and because he needed to get home to his wife. When Ben was gone, Ida Mae took the opportunity to dig deep into Brenda's life, all the while keeping the drinks flowing. She learned as much as she could about the heavy-hearted, kind woman. They both shared their hurtful stories, Brenda's being true and sincere, and Ida Mae being skewed here and there to suit the situation. After about 4 hours, Ida Mae was comfortable enough to trust that Brenda was not a spy and had no idea who she or Silky were. Brenda was harmless and was not connected with anyone who could hurt her. So, Ida Mae loosened up a bit. She told Brenda about Silky and about her not having any place to go. By 1:00 a.m., Ida Mae was paying $37 for a taxi back to Brenda's apartment in Brooklyn, one borough away from Queens, and a safe distance away from Silky. He knew Mae didn't know anyone like Brenda, and Mae intended to stay with Brenda for as long as she could. Brenda, on the other hand, had just met a nice woman who she thought could be an interesting new friend, possibly even a long-time companion. If nothing else, she was smoking hot and

Brenda was intrigued. She was just thrilled to be the one with whom Ida

Mae decided to leave.

Spinning A Wicked Web

In 1977, Donna Summer was cooing 'I Feel Love', everyone was working up a sweat to Marvin Gaye's 'Gotta Give It Up' and the Commodores were paying homage to all the sisters who were proud to show off their thick sexiness with 'Brick House'. It was a great time for free expression, partying and having fun. But, not everyone was enjoying themselves.

Brenda introduced Mae to her daughters in a girlish voice, as if she was asking her parents' permission to have a sleepover. The worry on her face said 'Please be the good, polite girls I know you are because I reaaallly need to impress her.' Mae was dressed a little too sexy for early in the morning, and too revealing to be visiting someone else's home (especially one with kids). They all thought "What kind of person would leave their home dressed this way?" Little did they know, Mae WAS home. Brenda had already moved her in, and didn't bother to ask them how they felt about it. It was a done deal. Her "nice to meet you" smile was sinister, and they immediately noticed how much power she had over their mother. Summer looked to her big sisters for answers, but they looked just as confused. They all said polite hellos, and nothing else. After introductions, they all went to their rooms and closed the door, and that was that.

If Mae was going to stay for a while, Brenda knew she would need to at least give the girls a heads up. So, the next morning Brenda coordinated another impromptu family meeting and announced (a little more firmly this time) that Mae would be staying with them for a while. For this meeting, Mae wore a shiny red Chinese robe with embroidery down the sides, a fluffy, long, curly wig, and matching furry slides with a 4 inch clear heel.

Brenda had gotten her statement out, and she was praying there wouldn't be any questions. There were none. Sabrina, Cheresse, Karla and Summer thought their mother had completely lost her mind. She had brought people home before, but she never, ever moved anyone in so ceremoniously. Brenda adjourned the meeting with "Ok" then made a quick exit with Mae back to her bedroom and closed the door. The girls looked at each other dumfounded, then quietly disbursed to their respective bedrooms and closed the doors without saying a word.

Mae wanted to live the life of a movie star. She took on the persona of the women she'd seen on television, from movies and those she'd grown up swooning over in the Hollywood Trade Magazines, like Lana Turner, Marilyn Monroe and Mae West (her idol). The long, sheer, movie star robes with feathers and fur around the collars and wrists, with matching satin furry slides and clear, acrylic heels on her feet. Brenda thought she was glamorous and was fascinated by her. She knew Mae looked like a hooker, but that was part of what she liked about her. She was risqué and didn't care what people thought of her. She oozed confidence and raw sexuality. And Brenda was still finding hers.

Mae slid and glided around the small Brooklyn apartment in her inappropriate attire, which was awkward for the girls. From body-suffocating cat suits to red teddies sheer at the nipples with matching thong panties and elegant, long sheer robes, nothing was off limits in her loungewear collection. Mae was unapologetically immodest. But, the girls weren't raised around nudity, or in hypersexual environments. Up until then, Brenda had kept such things behind closed doors, or outside of the house. So, to be thrown into such a 'free' space, where there were rules for everyone except Mae, was scary and confusing for them. Although Brenda was aware of these facts, she was not going to stop being who she was anymore. She was going to live her life now, and no one was going to tell her what she could and could not do anymore.

Brenda started ordering her daughters to do little things, like fixing them snacks, getting up to turn the television channel, and running small errands. Not a big deal, but Brenda had never regularly asked them to do these things in the past and she felt guilty. She had never had this much money at her disposal before to send them on regular errands either. Mae convinced her that they were kids and they SHOULD want to do things for their mother. If Mae had a taste for Haagen Daaz ice cream, Golden Circles bread or Pepsi, she said they should go to the store to get it. She kept wads of money and large packets of raw marijuana on their dresser, just thrown haphazardly, and she used these things as a means of controlling Brenda. It worked. She had been trying to raise four daughters on welfare checks, and was still struggling. And she never had extra money left over for the drugs she loved. But, with Mae, she didn't have to struggle anymore, her daughters had food, clothes and she had lots of drugs every day.

For the first few months, Mae was cordial and tried to be friendly toward Brenda and her daughters. She would try to win them over with gifts. She seemed to be playing the role of the new, loving step-dad. Sabrina and Cheresse saw through Mae's bribes and trickery, and they didn't make any secret of letting her know by the looks on their faces and attitudes that they didn't trust her nor would they tolerate her. They could not express themselves verbally out of respect for Brenda, but Brenda almost dared them to say anything to her directly. They stayed out of the house when they could, but when they had to be at home and near Mae they rolled their eyes, and gave Mae the silent treatment.

They couldn't understand it. Brenda had always been pretty tough. She was loving with them but strict. They had watched her go toe-to-toe with Jimmy. So, they knew she could handle herself if she had to. But, the person she was transforming into didn't seem like that same person. She seemed soft, and weak, like she didn't want to be in charge anymore. On the other hand, Mae was happy to take the reins.

When the fighting began, the girls really didn't know how to react. Mae picked fights with Brenda for any imaginary reason, i.e., something of hers was missing and she accused Brenda or her daughters of taking it. Brenda would have to defend herself and her kids, and look high and low for the items until it was found. Mae would scream, shout, stomp and slam lots of doors (her favorite way to express her anger). She would stomp around the apartment referring to the girls as "bitches" who were jealous of her and always "taking her shit." She would complain that Brenda wasn't disciplining them enough, and called them too wild. Mae said the older ones were at boy-crazy ages and told Brenda she needed

to 'break them' before it was too late. Brenda knew what Mae was doing.

She knew her daughters would never steal from anyone, or maliciously

move Mae's things (no matter how much they hated her). They were

good girls and simply weren't raised that way. But, she had to keep Mae

happy. She couldn't afford for her to leave. She enjoyed getting high

with Mae and the sex was great. Mae was like a wild cat in bed, a very

aggressive and adventurous lover, which Brenda had never experienced

before. She just had to do a better job of managing the situation.

At first, Brenda stood up to Mae and insisted her daughters were good

girls. When that strategy failed, Mae would claim to have seen Sabrina

and Cheresse talking to boys from the window, or some boy was trying

to touch them in inappropriate ways. Brenda never believed Mae, but

had to keep the peace. She said she would give them a good talking to.

But, Mae became relentless. She kept accusing them of things they

weren't doing and drove a wedge between Brenda and her daughters.

This was part of Mae's plan all along. Everyone in the house stopped

talking to each other. Before Mae, the girls could go into Brenda's room

and watch television with her, or just talk, sit with her and read, crack

jokes, whatever. She wasn't a perfect mother before, but they at least

knew she loved and cared about them and they loved her.

Brenda's bedroom door was now closed and locked 24-hours-a-day, letting the girls know that it was Mae's domain now and they were no longer welcome. It was also a way for Mae to isolate Brenda from her daughters, so she would feel hopeless and would only depend on Mae. Instead of trying to communicate with her daughters and repair the damage that was plaguing the family, Brenda got high. She got high all the time. Either she was high, or she was asleep, or she was out with Mae.

Sabrina and Cheresse shared a room, as did Karla and Summer. The sisters were like strangers living in the same apartment. They all kept their doors closed. Any time there was no fighting going on, it was eerily quiet in the apartment. The walls were very thin between the apartments, so the neighbors could clearly hear the fights, even without propping a glass against the wall and pressing their ears against the bottom (which was always the best way to hear fights through walls).

Naturally, Mae hated for their doors to be closed. She told Brenda "How you gonna let those bitches run your house like that?" Brenda would try to ignore her. "You aint gonna do nothin' about this shit?! They are being defiant, you don't see that?!" Brenda tried "No they're not. They just like to keep their doors closed. They aren't hurting anyone." Mae fought on "This is BULLSHIT. I PAY THE BILLS UP IN HERE." Next thing you know, Brenda would come out of her room, swing their doors open as wide as they could go, look at them with almost pleading eyes, saying nothing (as if to say "please don't close the doors again and make trouble for me"), then she would go back into her room and close the door. There was no real reason for it except that Mae wanted to show them she was in control of everyone in the house. She got off on it. Brenda went along with it, and the girls had no power to do anything about it. It was her way of letting them know she was their 'New Daddy'.

After a year, Sabrina and Cheresse started to rebel and closing their door anyway. This was one of the first incidences that set Mae on a path to destroy them. Mae would come out of the room, see their door closed, then swing it open wide and fast to startle them. She wanted to catch them doing something, and wanted to let them see her face. She would roll her eyes, and then close the door slowly to the halfway point, then walk away. It was juvenile, an intimidation tactic. She wanted to incite them, make them say something to her, battle her. Her whole life was about gaming people, acting, and pretending, for men, for money, or to just get her own way. She was manipulative, vicious, cunning, and ruthless, and she wasn't going to let anyone get in her way, not her ex-pimp, not Brenda, and certainly not her kids.

When Brenda and Mae weren't at home, Sabrina and Cheresse discussed and questioned the situation in their room. "Why doesn't Mommy apologize for letting Mae talk to us like that?" "She thinks she's somebody's Mother. She ain't MY Mother!" "No, she THINK she's somebody's DADDY, that's what she thinks... well, I have a Daddy." "Why doesn't Mommy kick that bitch out? She doesn't even seem to like Mommy all that much anyway, they fight all the time!" They agreed, Mae was dangerous and she needed to get out. Karla and Summer did not comment, just listened. They looked to their older sisters for help, for answers. But, they were just as baffled. They had survived divorce, being uprooted from all their friends in Queens, being poor, and moving to a new neighborhood. All they could do is try to look out for each other. They would continue to be respectful of their mother, even though she didn't deserve their respect anymore. They would just have to watch each other's backs.

Mae was formulating a plan to recruit Sabrina and Cheresse into her illegal activities. She was going to either force Brenda to use her two eldest daughters to work her department store shoplifting operation (which was her professional trade), or force them into prostitution (which would give her 'Pimp Status'). Brenda was adamant about preventing this from happening. She would allow Mae to exploit her, but not her daughters. This infuriated Mae, because she had invested a lot of time and money into twisting and bending Brenda's mind, and manipulating her in so many directions over the past year that Brenda believed Mae loved her and her daughters. When there was no fighting, she would come home with all sorts of (stolen) gifts of pretty new clothes, shoes, accessories, handbags, whatever she hadn't planned to sell, she would give to the girls. She used these things to bribe them and make them believe she cared. But, when she became angry, she would demand them back or they would find them shredded in the garbage can. It was all a huge game for Mae, and Mae <u>always</u> won. But, for some reason she could not push Brenda past the point where she would let Mae do whatever she wanted with them. So, Mae found other ways to make them miserable.

At 17 and 16 respectively, Mae told Brenda that Sabrina and Cheresse were too young to date, and they should not be allowed to have boyfriends. She said no boys should be calling the apartment, and they should not be able to stay out past curfew, not even in the summer when there was no school. At first, Brenda would give them permission to do things that Mae had already tried to sabotage, like going to a girlfriend's house or going to an underground jam outside with friends, which was something all the teenagers in the neighborhood did. If Mae would see them on the payphone outside or sitting on a bench talking to a boy (alone or in a group), she would walk over to them, right in front of their friends and ask "what choo think you doin?" They would boldly tell her "Mommy said I could be here." She would walk away, brooding. Like clockwork, Mae would go straight upstairs or straight to their bedroom and slam the door really hard. At first, it was funny to see her get so mad, and stomp off like a child. But, after a while those fits became fists that were blacking Brenda's eyes.

Battle for Control

Powerless, the girls tried to ignore the fact that their mother was being abused. The arguments started with a mixture of shouting and muffled noises. It was hard to make out who was hushing whom. Then the loud cursing and insults came "Your stupid ass, letting your whore daughters run around fucking these boys in the stairwells. You know they 'aint virgins no more!" This would infuriate Brenda, because she knew that wasn't true, and she didn't like anyone talking bad about her daughters. "Don't say that shit about my daughters" trying to sound tough, but muffling her voice to cue Mae to lower her own voice. This only incited Mae more "I'll say whatever the fuck I want to say. I pay the bills up in this house. Those bitches are eating the food "I" buy. I'm the only hoe in here turning high priced tricks." "Why do you always have to be so mean and nasty? Brenda whispered. "My daughters haven't done nothing wrong to you." Mae responded, "You don't like the way I talk about them, huh? You gonna choose them over me?" Mae would say in an innocent little girl voice. Then, Mae would bring her voice down low and ominous "Whatcha gonna do about it?" Silence. Then, the sound of shoving would ensue, the wheels on the bottom of the bed screeching

across the floor, perfume bottles being knocked over and breaking onto

the floor, bodies crashing into walls with a loud 'thud'. The sound of

two people struggling and wresting could be heard, "Don't pull my

hair!!!" "Dammit, you scratched me, Bitch!" Then muffled noises again.

Then silence. Then the dense sound of punching, fist against skin, in

fleshy and then in bony places, more slamming against the adjacent

bedroom walls, more furniture moving, more things falling and then

breaking against the tiled floor. Then long, long pauses of silence. Only

the voices of the television could be heard. Frightened, the girls didn't

know whether Brenda was ok, alive, hurt, or dead. Usually, Mae would

beat Brenda up, and rarely Brenda would get the better of Mae. The girls

prayed for the latter. Either way, it sounded as if somebody was getting

killed, and Brenda knew it had to be terrifying for her daughters. But,

what could she do?

Eventually, one of them would emerge from the room first, usually

Brenda, going straight into the bathroom, sniffling, and trying to hold her

head high despite the obvious embarrassment. They exhaled when they

saw their mother walk out of the room… no limping sound, no

whimpering, no labored breathing. They'd be afraid to look her way as she passed their doorway. She would hurry to close the bathroom door, turn on the faucet all the way so the water was loud and beating hard against the porcelain. She didn't want them to hear her crying, but they knew she was. She would clean up her battered eye or bloody nose. She would fill the red rubber water bottle with cold water to soothe her bruises, then open the squeaky, sliding cabinet door above the toilet. She'd shake two aspirins out of the bottle, and pop them into her mouth to help ease any swelling, aches and pains that she knew were coming when she woke up the next morning. More often than not there was a black eye or a scratch on her face. Mae was like an alley cat and went straight for Brenda's face, because she wanted her to be embarrassed to go out in public that way. She wanted her friends to see her that way, and she wanted her to try to lie about it. She wanted them all to know that Brenda was hers, and she could do whatever she wanted with her and to her. Brenda wore sunglasses when she went outside, to hide her shame, and to cover her black eyes.

Mae rarely ever went to clean up after the fights. She always had very few bruises or cuts anywhere. When Mae did have a bruise or two on her light skin, it was so small she could cover it with makeup, or she could wear an accessory to hide it. Mae would mainly go into the kitchen and make herself something to eat after the fights. As if she had just worked up a hearty appetite. She would make a sandwich, or heat up some chicken and fried rice, or make a bowl of Haagen Daaz Chocolate Ice Cream.

One day, when Mae was not around and Brenda was feeling especially vulnerable with the girls, she felt motivated to explain away the abuse she was enduring. She told them "Mae's mother was a mean lady, and she used to fight with Mae when she was a little girl. Then she had to fight off men in the entertainment industry who made her promises they didn't keep. And then she had to fight off boyfriends (she didn't want to say pimps). And then she had to fight her mother for not protecting her. She doesn't mean anything with the things she says. All she knows how to do is fight." It was clear Brenda wasn't looking for a dialogue about it. It was more for her than for them. She wanted them to believe Mae's behavior was something families go through, normal, natural, and necessary things, and that they somehow should try to understand her. They didn't understand any of it.

They thought about calling the police on Mae. They knew the police were looking for her. It would have been so easy. But, then, if they did that, Brenda would go, too. And, who knows what would happen to them then? They were more afraid of Mae than the police. What if she found out, and then tried to kill them in their sleep? What if she walked out of that bedroom one day with blood all over her, and announced that their mother was dead? They couldn't have that happen. So, they decided against it.

Mae succeeded in bringing Brenda down to a docile state, suppressing her will to fight. She had to face her few friends with black eyes and bruises on her body. Mae was sadistic. She would send her on an errand to her friend's house on purpose, to sell clothes and collect money. And, she knew if Brenda decided to go on an interview or tried to get a job, she wouldn't keep it very long if she showed up black and blue. Someone would ask questions, or call the police.

The rare times Brenda would acknowledge the beatings, she would assure her daughters that she was not really hurt, and that she was okay. She didn't want them to worry, despite her obvious pain. She wanted them to believe she had the situation all under control. But, it was clear she had no control over what was happening to her, or to them, and she had no idea how to get out of her situation.

Temptress

Once Mae fell asleep, Brenda would turn the volume on the tv set all the way down. She could hear the girls whispering, and sometimes the muffled sound of tears in a pillow. Most of the time she couldn't go right out of the room after the fights. It was too embarrassing. The whispering stopped, and the crying stopped, too. Sabrina and Cheresse would turn on their record player, which seemed to help drown out the sound. But, Mae thought the loud music was a sign of disrespect. She would bust open their door without any warning, stare at them and dare them to say something with her eyes, then walk away leaving the door wide open out of spite.

Karla and Summer weren't so lucky, as they had no tv or record player in their room. They did have a clock radio, and that did help to deflect the banging, slapping and punching sounds. They waited out the brawls, holding their breath to make sure it was over, and prayed hard for the door to open with Brenda walking out alive, and Mae finally dead.

On New Year's Eve, Mae decided she and Brenda should go out on the town, and ring in the New Year right. She contacted some friends and arranged for VIP transportation and a special table at an elite club in Queens owned by an associate of hers. It had been one whole year since Mae set foot in Queens, and she was feeling confident she could do so without anyone alerting Silky. She brought home an outfit for Brenda to wear: 3-piece, white pantsuit with expensive round toed navy leather boots, and a royal blue silk shirt. Silk had always made Brenda sweat and Mae knew it. Although she wasn't looking forward to sweating all night, she said "Thank you" and put on the outfit.

At the party, Mae and Brenda danced, laughed, drank, and for the first time in a long while, Brenda remembered the feeling she had when she first met Mae. When she talked to her about life, and her childhood, and her innermost thoughts and feelings. They were enjoying the party, and had counted down to the New Year together. With the exception of her having to excuse herself to the restroom so that she could shove tissue paper underneath her arms to soak up the sweat, she was having a ball. She stopped at the bar on her way back to the table to get a beer for herself and a Chivas for Mae. A woman Brenda had never seen before came over to the bar and ordered a Vodka Tonic, then struck up a conversation. "Happy New Year Beautiful," she said. She was a tall, caramel-colored sister with two long braids at either side of her head. The braids were sparkling with glitter and gems for the festive occasion. Brenda gave her a friendly smile "Hi, Happy New Year to you, too." She cautiously peeked over at Mae, who was being entertained by two men grinning hungrily down at her huge breasts protruding out of her shimmering silver studded sheath dress, showing every curve on her body. They hovered over Mae, enjoying the view, and begging to be invited to sit. Turning her attention back to the woman, who extended her hand and said, "I'm Candy." Brenda responded, "Brenda, nice to meet you Candy." Over the music, Candy asked with a smile "You here with someone, or you bringing in '78 alone like me?" Brenda picked up the two drinks and was about to decline Candy's obvious impending invitation, when Mae appeared out of nowhere and punched Candy in the face so hard she crumbled down to the floor between two barstools. Brenda jumped back and the drinks fell to the floor, Mae's glass of Chivas shattered. "What in the hell did you do that for???" yelled Brenda (barely audible over the music). "I'm not trying to have this" said Mae. "Have WHAT? She was just saying hello!" "Dammit, Mae…You don't own me" said Brenda, regretting the words as soon as they were out of her mouth. Mae balled up her fists and was about to strike, when the owner of the club Jimmy Robinson grabbed Mae by both arms, looked her in the eyes, and quietly asked her to leave his establishment so everyone else can enjoy their New Year's Eve celebration. He wasn't really asking. He whispered in Mae's ear, "I'll take care of Candy, Go."

When they got outside, Brenda was trying to hail a cab, and Mae was screaming at her, calling her "Whore" and "Bitch" and "Stupid Piece of Shit." She stepped out into the street and raised her arm "TAXI!" Mae followed, trying to keep the fight going, shoving Brenda and daring her to hit her. Brenda walked around her, trying to avoid her, and pretending to be solely focused on securing that taxi. A cab finally stopped, but was reluctant to take her with Mae yelling and cursing behind her. He said "Is 'she' coming too?" Brenda said in a low voice so Mae couldn't hear her over her yelling "No." He told her to get in, which she did. Mae didn't try to get in with her. Instead, she hurled her purse at the cab as it pulled away. Drunk and angry as hell, Mae screamed after her "YOU NEED ME, BITCH. I DON'T NEED YOU!"

Mae didn't come back home for five days. Brenda didn't know where she went, and she really didn't care. The first night she was on pins and needles. She spent half of the night praying Mae wouldn't come back to Brooklyn. She fantasized about packing her things and shipping them to her friend Barbara at the address Mae had given her in case of any real emergency. When she woke up and Mae wasn't lying next to her, she prayed for it again the next night and it came true. On the third day, her daughters were noticeably more relaxed than they had been in two years, and so was she. They didn't ask where Mae was, or whether she was coming back. It was as if no one wanted to summon the evil by talking about her. The girls just kept their routines, went to school, dance class, after school program, as they always did, like normal. On day four, at 11am when the girls were at school and Brenda was all alone, the phone rang, and it was Mae. She told Brenda she had been so depressed because she missed her son who was living in South Carolina with her mother, and she knows she's been acting really crazy lately. It was her way of apologizing, without actually apologizing. She asked Brenda if she could come and get a few things from the apartment. Reluctantly, Brenda agreed. She arrived wearing a painted-on leopard print one-piece cat suit barely snapped shut from just below her navel up to the top of her rib cage. No panties. Tall black patent leather boots. She was carrying an expensive box of chocolates in the shape of a heart. It was her version of a peace offering, all of it. One hour later, Brenda was curled up with Mae in their bed, high on midday marijuana and Chivas Regal.

The Art of Flanking

Peace was a fleeting memory just 24-hours later when Mae announced it was time for them to get back out there to work. Mae was especially controlling when it came to business transactions. Demands of her shoplifting hustle had picked up and she couldn't afford to go it alone anymore.

She was constantly honing her craft, staking out stores and surveillance procedures. She had a new scheme and she was going to need Brenda's help.

She said Brenda had to go to work with her if she wanted them to have enough money to keep food in the house, pay the rent, keep the phone on, etc. Brenda was hesitant at first, telling Mae "I'm no criminal, I wouldn't even know what to do out there." Mae said, "I'll teach you! It's a piece of cake. The key is to be smart about it." Brenda did everything she could to avoid going, but Mae began to get angry and violent again, so Brenda relented. She was scared out of her mind that she would get arrested, and was deathly afraid of going to jail, especially after all the horror stories she had heard over the years. She was a good girl, she told herself. What would Kate do if she ever found out? She shuddered at the thought. What would happen to her kids if she was arrested? She couldn't think about that right now.

They would head out early in the morning to make their rounds at high-end department stores like Macy's Herald Square, Bloomingdale's and Lord & Taylor in Midtown, and, at that time Gimbals Department Store. They would do something called "flanking". Flanking was a shoplifting scheme in which clothes would be taken from one area of the store and moved to another area to store them for pick up later. In Mae's case, this area was usually the furniture department. Clothes could be quickly stashed under a couch or bed until collection. Several trips would take place throughout the day. She would return to the furniture department later with empty shopping bags, and exit the stores as if she had purchased all the items. This was before department stores got smart and affixed metal sensors on clothing. Mae would have a man she knew positioned outside of the store in a parked car. She would get in with her multiple bags and he would drive her away to safety. Two trips were usually scheduled per day. Mae said this process would be a lot faster and less conspicuous if Brenda did it with them.

The first time Brenda flanked with Mae was at Bloomingdales. She was very nervous, and sweating, she called too much attention to herself and got caught. The security guard saw her looking suspicious roaming around the furniture department, not looking as if she was buying anything, and when he saw her walking out of the store with a shopping bag he became suspicious and asked her to go with him into the back room to chat. Mae had already made her way to the car and was waiting. After 10 minutes, Mae told her driver to take off because Brenda's stupid ass probably got caught. She phoned her lawyer in Manhattan, Mr. Rubenstein, who she paid $5,000 in cash to get the charges reduced against Brenda. She spent the night in jail, and was out on bail the next day, receiving a warning, as a first-time offender.

The second time out they hit Lord & Taylor. Brenda never made it out of the store before she was spotted and interrogated. She never gave Mae up to the police and insisted she acted alone. They didn't buy it, but they had nothing else to go on. They charged her with possession of stolen property. Mr. Rubenstein got her off with a two-year probation.

Brenda was terrified each time she went flanking, but she worked up her nerve and actually got better at it. They continued flanking, staying away from the previous stores they had hit, but instead targeted Gimbals and the Lord & Taylor in Nassau and Suffolk counties where their pictures weren't posted up in the back of the stores.

They brought home designer dresses, sweaters, pants, coats, shoes, hats, just about anything. Mae would use all kinds of disguises for flanking. She would dress up like a nurse. She dressed up like a nun, but only with the head dressing, not the full habit. She was also a schoolteacher. She would pull her hair back into a tight bun, slip on a long skirt, sweater and glasses, too. Her game was definitely tight. They would sell a lot of the clothes to Brenda's friends and neighbors at reduced prices. Brenda would get some clothes out of the deal as well. Mae wanted her 'girl' to look good, so she selected things she liked to see on Brenda. They brought back clothes for the girls, too. They were always the best designer dresses, and outfits for school, for the older girls' silk blouses, designer slacks, boots, you name it. This was the only plus to being nice to her. She even got Kate a long, pale pink satin robe with fur around the collar for Christmas. Brenda wrapped it up and presented it to Kate in a gift box from her and Mae, and reluctantly, Kate accepted it. She took it up to her room to try it on over her leisure slacks and button-down blouse. She descended the stairs, and everyone made a huge deal about how fabulous she looked. Brenda beamed with pride and found comfort in this rare moment where everyone was light-hearted, and no one was focused on her failures in life.

Take Down

Anytime Brenda and Mae exited and entered the apartment building together, there was an uneasy tension between them and the rest of the residents, like the couple were carrying a secret that everybody knew. But, nobody said anything out loud. They would stare, and then lean over talking in muffled tones as Brenda and Mae passed. Most often Brenda went through the back entrance, where there was no foot traffic, and one could go up in the elevator undetected by all except the security guard. But, Mae loved the spotlight and insisted on walking through the front of the building. She was always dressed in high fashion, flashy clothes, handbags, expensive wigs, high heeled shoes, full make-up, and low-cut dresses. She always took every opportunity to show off her large breasts and cleavage. She was her own billboard and she knew how to sell her merchandise.

When Brenda's eyes were swollen, she walked in and out of the building, trying to look cool and confident, but hardly speaking to people she'd known for years, because of Mae. In contrast, on the good days, she would be overly friendly in her wave to long-time friends Vera and

Regina, who just might be outside. They waved back "Hey Brenda!" but

wouldn't say much else, because they knew that if Mae didn't stop to

chat, then neither could Brenda. If Mae had an especially good score

that week or that day, she would be dripping with department store

shopping bags filled with boosted items. She had a good hustle going,

since there were 4 other buildings on the complex just like theirs. She

did the math in her mind the first night Brenda brought her home: 26 x

17 = 442 apartments, and 442 apartments x 5 buildings is 2,210

apartments filled with families that like designer clothes, shoes, bags,

belts, hats, jewelry, wallets, perfume, which they ordinarily would never

be able to afford. Mae made it possible to look good 'on the cheap.'

Usually, sales went as smoothly as planned. If they were Brenda's

friends they could come to their apartment to buy. But, if they had just

heard about Mae's business, she went to them. She carried knives and

always had one or two small handguns on her person at all times, in case

something went down. So, although Brenda's friends and neighbors

hated Mae, and knew she was abusive and dangerous, they would smile

in her face and make friends with her, because they wanted desperately

to become and remain 'good customers,'

One day in the Spring of 1979, Sabrina was in her room getting ready for a trip to Coney Island beach with her boyfriend Dorian. Cheresse was lying on her bed flipping through a magazine. Mae in her black, satin Chinese robe and matching red satin high-heeled slippers stepped into her doorway and said to Sabrina, "And just where in the hell do you think you going?" Sabrina said, "I'm going OUT with my friends." Mae turned up her lips and snarled nastily, "You aint goin' nowhere." Sabrina whipped around and said, "My mother said I could go out, and I'm going." Mae replied, "Well, 'I' said you aint goin' nowhere, and you aint!" Fuming, Sabrina stayed in her room for hours trying to decide whether she should sneak out of the house or avoid a fight. She pretended not to care, but was secretly still plotting how to get out of the house. She didn't show it on her face or in her actions, but she had decided to go. Trying to diffuse the fast-approaching storm, Brenda stepped into Sabrina and Cheresse's doorway, with pleading eyes, and asked Sabrina if she wanted to go to Coney Island beach with her and Mae. Brenda thought it sounded like a good solution, and would satisfy all parties involved. Having just about enough as she could stand, Sabrina rolled her eyes and said "No, I want to go out with my friend like you said I could." Mae pushed past Brenda and said, "You ungrateful little bitch. Just for that, now you aint goin' nowhere, AND you on punishment, too!" Brenda's eyes dropped to the floor in defeat.

She quietly turned around and went into her bedroom, deciding to search

for a rolled joint on her cluttered dresser. "I'm going out with my friends.

You are NOT my mother, and you can't tell me what to do!" seethed

Sabrina. She pushed past Mae and ran out of the apartment and down

three floors to her boyfriend Dorian's family's apartment. She was

fuming with anger as she told Dorian what was going on. Once he

calmed her down, she told him to meet her back downstairs in the lobby

so they could go to the beach. Dorian, who was well aware of the volatile

situation, told his mother Cynthia what was going on.

Cynthia had a strong, intimidating presence. She had seven sisters, and they all lived nearby in Brooklyn with their families. They were a very large, close-knit family who stuck together. The sisters were very vocal, and ran their households (and their careers) with a firm grip. No man had ever beat them or abused them verbally, and certainly not physically. The only thing they feared was God.

She had gotten to know Sabrina as she spent time with her son, and had even become very good friends with her two daughters, too. She spent lots of time with their family, and often ate meals at their home.

Cynthia was very influential in the community, and could use that influence to deliver Sabrina and her sisters from their living situation if she wished, including report certain illegal activities to the proper authorities. But, she couldn't raise red flags, or risk having the kids being removed from the household and placed into the care of social services. They weren't being physically abused, and Sabrina had assured her they were ok for the most part.

Brenda couldn't tell Cynthia that she admired her strength and her determination, and the fierce way she protected her children. That would be admitting she wasn't. Secretly, she wished Cynthia or anyone would do what she was too afraid to do... even if it meant she might have to go, too.

Sabrina headed back upstairs. Mae and Brenda were sitting on the living room couch, with Brenda pretending to watch tv. She walked past them and went into her bedroom without speaking and closed the door. Brenda kept smoking her cigarette and staring forward blankly at the tv. Mae had stared Sabrina down as she passed by, daring her to say something, mad now that she didn't. Sabrina emerged from her bedroom a few minutes later with a small backpack, "I'm going to the beach with my friends," she said and started making her way to the door. Mae jumped up and followed her, "You are not." "I hate you!" Sabrina shot back. "If you hate me so much" said Mae, "then gimme back allllaMYYYshiiiit." Sabrina shouted "I will!" stomping back to her bedroom and emptying all her drawers and her closet with everything

Mae ever gave her. Dresses, skirts, pocketbooks, hair dryer, bathrobe, shoes, everything. It was all in a pile in front of Brenda and Mae's bedroom door, blocking the walkway. Then she picked up her backpack and headed for the door. Brenda sat like a zombie, blowing smoke, and pretending there was something far more interesting on tv. Mae almost broke her neck when her high-heeled, leopard slipper got caught in the pile of clothes as she hurried behind Sabrina yelling, "Get back here!" Sabrina stood in front of the tv and faced her mother "What is wrong with you???!!! You can't even make decisions for yourself anymore??! I thought you were supposed to be the man?!!!" Mae hauled off and slapped Sabrina across the face, her heavy silver ring cutting into her cheek and was now bleeding. Sabrina touched her stinging face, saw the blood on her fingers and with all the rage and hate inside of her body, she jumped on top of Mae like a wild dog. She began punching her in her face and arms. Mae was blocking her with her hands and calling her a crazy bitch. Hearing the commotion, Cheresse shot out of the back room and into the living room. Seeing the fight, she jumped on top of Mae too, clawing at her face and hair. Mae was like a crazed, rabid street cat, clawing after the girls trying to grab their hair and going straight for the face. Karla and Summer ran into the living room and watched as their sisters knocked over the glass coffee table, and sections of the couch came undone. Brenda was shoved toward the terrace door and onto the floor as hair was being pulled out, and the years of built-up frustrations of two teenage girls attacked Mae from every direction. She was screaming and cursing at everyone, and demanding that Brenda "get these bitches" off of her. Mae fighting for her life and scratching around like a wild alley cat was surreal, but also frightening and exhilarating for Summer. She and Karla wanted to join, but were too afraid of the repercussions afterward. Summer secretly wished her sisters would kill Mae. At the time it seemed like a good thing to wish. Karla wouldn't get into the physical sparring, but she was yelling at the top of her lungs "GET HER! GET HER!" Brenda finally woke from her trance and made a weak effort to break up the fight.

Karla ran down the hall to their neighbor Vanessa's house and banged fast and hard on the door. Vanessa hurriedly swung the door open "What's wrong, Karla??!!" "THEY FIGHTIN'!" said Karla. She explained quickly and then asked, "Can I call my Nana?"

Sabrina spat on the floor next to Mae, "Don't you EVER put your hands on me again!" then rushed out of the house bleeding from the face and looking like she had been in a bar room brawl. She stormed past Summer as she picked up her bag and headed out of the apartment, slamming the door behind her. Cheresse wriggled herself free from Brenda's hands, gave Mae the evil eye, went to her room and slammed her door. This time she locked it. Brenda pretended to help Mae up from the floor. She slapped her hands away, fixing her clothes, wiping her face, and catching her breath. Karla and Summer now stood against the living room wall, staring at Mae who looked a mess. Her wig was across the room hiding underneath the radiator, her gown was in tatters and hanging lopsided from her body. She was wearing one slipper and looking for the other one under the couch. Her breasts were falling out of her gown and she had to hold it with her hands to keep it from falling completely off. Her short pressed (real) hair was all over her head and she was rubbing the red bruises on the legs and arms. Brenda pretended to fuss over her, trying to help her up and calm her down. She wasn't speaking, but her face was in a rage. "Oh yeah? That's how it's gonna be, huh?" She said out loud but really to herself. "Ok... ok... I got somethin' for their asses." She passed the girls, rolling her eyes hard at Karla, whose eyes were now dropped to the floor.

Karla was scared she would get into trouble for betting against Mae. She and Summer went into their bedroom and closed the door. Brenda followed Mae into their bedroom and softly closed their door as well.

Mae was leaning over the dresser and examining her face in the mirror, "Shit". She took off the tattered gown and threw it into the trash. She stood there for a moment, naked, checking herself out. She could see Brenda's reflection in the mirror, checking her out too, but trying to pretend she wasn't. She knew Brenda was scared. She hadn't done anything to protect Mae from that attack. She glared at Brenda. She had to give them girls a little credit though, they had more fire than their mother.... That kind of fire could be useful, she thought. They just needed a good coach to use that to their advantage. She made mental notes. "Hmpf" she said under her breath. She went over to her closet and put on a ¾ camel-colored wrap dress, spike heeled tall cream-colored boots, snatched her long curly wig off the stand and arranged it onto her head. She took a deep breath, exhaled, began applying her make-up. Before she could grab her Louis Vuitton satchel to head out, the doorbell rang. Summer ran to the door (knowing full well who was there), and swung it open, throwing her little body up against her grandmother.

"Are you ok? Are you girls ok?!" "Yes, Nana" said Summer. Wearing navy polyester slacks, a tan button-down blouse, her square-toed, beige pleather loafers, and brown tapestry handbag over her shoulder and clutched tight under her right arm, she rushed into the living room. Obviously, she threw on the nearest wig, her least favorite, a tightly curled too-shiny black wig (little orphan 'Annie' style), which she had no time to pin down tightly because it was slightly off-center. She pulled her long sewing scissors out of her bag, point facing outward, and screamed toward the back of the apartment, "Brenda! Brenda, get your tail out here right now!!! And where's Mae?!" She quickly surveyed the living room, saw the ill-placed furniture, and coffee table magazines peeking from under the couch. She was furious, and disgusted at the same time.

Scrambling to her feet, Brenda panicked. She whispered "Oh Shit! What in the hell is she doing here?" "Your damn kids must have called her" said Mae calmly. "I'm not dealing with this bullshit today." Mae grabbed her bag, opened the bedroom door and was headed out. Brenda stumbled to get in front of Mae to reach her mother first. "Ma... I..." "SHUT UP BRENDA! This is all your fault anyway!" Kate turned her attention to Mae "MAE" pointing the scissors tight-fisted toward Mae's face "Don't you ever put your hands on MY kids again. These are NOT your kids!" Mae stood silently, almost ambivalent. Kate turned to Brenda "You'd better get yourself together, or else." Mae was secretly getting a kick out of seeing Brenda get told off by her mother, and tickled by this old lady thinking she could take her.

By now Cheresse and Karla were standing in the hallway, and came out to hug Kate. She pulled their chins up and looked at their faces "Are you *really* ok?" Their mouths said yes, but their eyes were pleading NO. Her heart broke for her beautiful grandbabies.

"Where is Sabrina?" Kate asked.

Cheresse said "Probably at her boyfriend's apartment." Kate found Sabrina outside in the back of the building talking with her boyfriend's mother Cynthia. She loosened the grip on her handbag and placed the scissors inside. "Are you hurt?" she asked Sabrina. "Yes" she cried hot, angry tears into her grandmother's blouse. Both Kate and Cynthia feeling helpless consoled her. They assured her everything would be ok, but they both had no idea whether that was actually possible. Once Kate felt comfortable that Sabrina was ok, she instructed her to call her later that night. Cynthia promised she would let Sabrina call later from her house. Kate thanked her and headed to her car.

Brenda went looking for Sabrina after Kate left. She found her still outside in the back of the building talking to Cynthia. She was tending to the cut on Sabrina's face. Brenda walked over cautiously and ordered Sabrina to go upstairs. Sabrina did not move. Brenda was already angry with Cynthia because she felt she encouraged Sabrina to defy her. She was the mother, and she did not take kindly to anyone undermining her authority when it came to her children (anyone except Mae, that is).

"You need to mind your business Cynthia. This is none of your

concern." Ignoring her statement, Cynthia said with the perfect mix of

intimidation and Southern charm, "Brenda, how could you let that

woman put her hands on your kids? It ain't right you letting her do that."

Embarrassed, but still trying to stand her ground, she ignored Cynthia's

statement "Go back upstairs Sabrina!" Unsure what to do, Sabrina didn't

move. She just knew she had enough of Mae, and she did not want to go

back up to that apartment. Reaching for Sabrina's arm, "COME... ON!

I don't have TIME for this!" Brenda gritted through her teeth. Sabrina

tore her arm away and screamed dramatically "I'm not going back up

there with you and that monster." Crying now, "Can't you see I'm

BLEEDING??! Look at my FACE!!! Don't you even care???" Cynthia

held Sabrina as she cried and after a few quiet moments, Brenda gave

up, turned around and went back upstairs. Sabrina buried her face in

Cynthia's chest balling her eyes out. She just couldn't understand why

her mother wouldn't do something about this awful situation. As the

eldest, she had always seen her mother as strong, smart and powerful.

She never seemed to take any crap from anyone, not even Jimmy. She

could be furious with him, tell him off on the phone, and wouldn't think

twice about doing it to his face, too. She was very stern and firm in raising her and her sisters, and for the most part, they were pretty fearful of any punishments for bad behavior. So, to see her in a submissive, abused role this way, allowing someone to beat her down physically and emotionally, and attack her daughters, made no sense to Sabrina at all.

Cynthia who was a devout woman, did not believe in pre-marital sex, and would never encourage her only son to 'shack up' with a girl. But, she could not sit idly by and see Sabrina in distress and homeless. So, Sabrina spent the night at Cynthia's apartment with her family, and she told her they would work out a plan the next day.

The next morning Cheresse snuck some of her clothes out of the house before Mae and Brenda woke up from their all-night reefer-smoking session, and took them to Cynthia's for Sabrina. There was a family discussion about house rules while Sabrina was there, and what would be the next move for helping Sabrina get settled someplace safe. Cynthia would help her find a job and help her get set up in an apartment (preferably with a roommate). She was, after all, only 18 years old. Cynthia was able to call in a few favors and secure Sabrina a job working with a non-profit city organization called the Summer Youth Program, which provided summer employment to inner-city kids.

Sabrina started her first *real* job as a staff coordinator for Summer

Youth the following week. Of course, since she had to get a full-time job in order to save her money and get her own apartment, this required her to drop out of her freshman year in college. She stayed with Cynthia and her family for five months before the plan took shape. The whole time she prayed she would not run into Mae or Brenda going in and out of the building, or up or down in the elevator. She wasn't afraid of them. She just thought it would be awkward, and she didn't know exactly how crazy Mae would behave in public. So, she avoided them. In truth, Mae hadn't intended to cause any scenes in public. She wasn't going to call any added attention to herself at that time, because the police had already gotten too close for her comfort. Sabrina never crossed paths with Brenda or Mae during her months at Cynthia's.

Six months from the day of the big fight with Mae, Sabrina moved into a two-bedroom apartment with her high school friend Denita, on South Elliot Place in the downtown area of Brooklyn. She was very worried about how her sisters would cope with Mae and Brenda in her absence, but she felt she owed it to herself to gain some normalcy in her life. This was going to be a new beginning for her, and she was looking forward to it.

So Close

One morning in October of 1979, Cheresse was up getting herself ready for her freshman classes at Brooklyn College. Karla was having her turn in the shower, and Summer was in the kitchen assembling a peanut butter and jelly sandwich for breakfast and packing her school bag. Brenda and Mae were sleeping off a night of partying, and whatever else they had been doing until the wee hours of the morning. The doorbell rang and startled Summer. No one had ever visited so early in the morning. Shep, the family's German Shepard, started barking loudly and repeatedly at the sound of the doorbell.

> *When Mae first brought Shep home as a puppy, the family wasn't going to keep him, because 1) no dogs were allowed in the apartments, and 2) Mae said she bought the dog for her son Neville who lived down south with her mother. Summer soon realized the dog was really brought in for Mae's own protection. She wanted to deter unwanted visitors, whether burglar, or pimp, or police. Whatever the reason, Mae and Brenda knew they were breaking the terms of the lease agreement, but they preferred to take their chances with exposure by the rent office vs. being arrested, robbed or killed without some security.*

Brenda had a favorite saying, "I'll deal with that when the time comes."

Summer had a butter knife in her hand and wasn't sure what to do. "Who is it?" she yelled. "It's the Police!" exclaimed the man on the other side of the door. Panicked, Summer yelled "Just a minute" and ran to the back bedrooms to get Cheresse. By now, the reality of the illegal dog barking like crazy was secondary to the more pressing matter of the police being at the door. The dog, feeding off of the quiet frenzy going on in the apartment, his large paws were tripping over the back of Summer's ankles. She whispered to Cheresse that the police were at the door. She knocked on her mother's bedroom door and told her the police were at the door. Mae jumped out of the bed in a panic, half-dressed in one of her revealing pink nighties, her huge breasts partially exposed, and flopping out of her lingerie. Brenda sat up in bed, eyes bulging, hair all over her head. She looked exhausted, and was either too impaired from her coke and weed-induced high, or she was just too confused to know what to do in the moment. Mae, on the other hand, tiptoed into the front of the apartment like a cat burglar, through the living room and through the other open end of the kitchen, furthest from the front door. Cheresse already knew her job would be to make the police go away. No words needed to be said between her and Mae. Mae quickly but quietly creaked opened the bottom cabinet door under the kitchen sink and squeezed her big behind inside, holding the lopsided cabinet door shut. This far from religious woman began to whisper a silent prayer. The doorbell rang again, followed by five hard knocks on the door. Cheresse rolled her eyes and said, in a calm, very collected, measured voice, through the door "Who is it?" Another male voice said "It's the police, please open the door." She looked over her shoulder at Summer, and motioned for her to go into the kitchen out of sight, hold onto the dog, and try to keep him quiet. She unlocked all three locks, and saw two white, male, uniformed police officers. The shorter of the two said, as he looked down at a clipboard, "We're looking forrrr Cheresse Taylor". Surprised, but without skipping a beat, she replied "I'm Cheresse Taylor." By now, Shep was barking and jumping around like crazy in the kitchen, scratching at the cabinet where Mae was hiding. Not thinking about her drugged-up mother in the back bedroom, Summer was secretly praying hard that the officers would ask to come in to see why the dog was barking, maybe look around the apartment. She knew that if they came inside and saw Shep barking at that cabinet like a lunatic, they would have most certainly discovered Mae and she would be gone from their lives forever. Officer #1 stood in the doorway looking at the clipboard again, looking at Cheresse, looking at his partner, then back at the clipboard. "That doesn't look like her" he said to his partner. Officer #2 shook his head in agreement. Officer # 1 turned the clipboard around for Cheresse to see. It was a mug shot of Mae. The officer said, "Do you know this woman or why she would be using your name?" Cheresse looked at the photo blankly and said, "No, I don't know who that is." More dog barking. Officer # 1 brought the clipboard down to his left side and said, "Sorry to have bothered you." And they turned and walked down the long hallway toward the elevators, watching them walk away without Mae was the most crushing bout of hopelessness Cheresse had ever felt, next to the day her dad had drove off with all his belongings. She had missed her opportunity to get revenge on Mae. She took her time closing the door. She locked all three locks, walked back to her bedroom to finish getting ready for school. She had a look of utter disgust on her face now. Summer knew she was fuming. Cheresse closed the bedroom door, grabbed her windbreaker jacket from her bed, and left for school.

Summer finally exhaled the breath she had been holding since Cheresse had opened the door, and walked over to the cabinet where Mae was still hiding. She told her it was okay to come out now. Mae squeezed out of the tiny cabinet covered with dust, dirt and roach droppings or whatever else was living down there in that barely used cabinet. Her wig was half off her head, and she looked flustered and scared. She was sliding her body along the walls, and peeping out of the front door's peep-hole to make sure the police were gone. She was as white as a ghost, and visibly shaken by the visit. She crawled across the living room couch, crawled on the floor and snatched the curtains closed so no one could see into the apartment through the glass windows and doors on the terrace. Then she practically crawled back to the bedroom, putting her finger up to her mouth to shush Summer, paranoid the apartment was now under surveillance. Summer had never been so entertained by the fear she had seen in Mae that day. She prayed to God and asked Him to bring the police back and arrest Mae. But, they never came. And she knew if they arrested Mae, they would have to arrest Brenda, too.

Mae didn't leave the house for three days after that incident. She kept whispering that it was 'too hot' for her to go outside.

Unseen

Everyone in the neighborhood knew the nature of Brenda and Mae's relationship. They knew Mae lived with Brenda and her daughters. They knew of Brenda and Mae's illegal activities. They knew Mae was abusive, and they also knew Mae was Brenda's lover. Summer knew that her mother did not have a traditional relationship like other women and mothers in the complex where they lived. Summer knew something secretive and different was going on behind their bedroom door, but she had no reason to try to clarify it at twelve years old. It was just done and that was that.

One day Summer had been outside playing and getting completely dirty and sweaty from double-dutch, freeze tag and relay races with her friends. Just after dark, Veronica 'Ronnie' Jenkins, Summer's next door neighbor and on again/off again friend, had met her quota for daily bullying. She had convinced Summer to go upstairs to her apartment and ask her mother for some money to buy Bon Ton potato chips and quarter juices for 'both of them' from Sutter Avenue. (Quarter juice came in little plastic containers shaped like barrels and costed 25 cents).

It was apparently Summer's turn to buy. The two girls rode the elevator to the tenth floor. When the elevator door opened they both bolted down the long hallway, racing to see who would reach the apartment door first, with Ronnie shoving the smaller-framed Summer, as she often did. "I WON!" Ronnie said laughing and breathing hard. "You cheated" said Summer. "I'm just faster" replied Ronnie. Summer took her keys from her pants pocket and opened the door. It was around 8:30 p.m., and it was a hot and sticky summer night. When they walked into the apartment, it was completely dark and, at first, it appeared that no one was home. The faint sound of a television could be heard from the back bedroom area, as a white light spread along the floor into the hallway. Summer knew that meant Brenda and Mae, or at least one of them, were in the room and likely asleep. At the living room, Summer whispered to Ronnie "Wait here" and then she tip-toed slowly to the back to avoid waking whoever might have been asleep. Her plan was to sneak into the room where they were sleeping, and take two dollars and some change off of the dresser, which she occasionally did. They always had change on the dresser, and didn't care if she took it as long as they knew about it. She decided she would tell them she took it in the morning, as it would be rude to wake them up. When she opened the door a crack, the first thing she saw was the light of the tv through the darkness. But, as she eased the door open wider, she could see the sheets moving around. Brenda and Mae hadn't heard the door open at first, but when it creaked at a 45-degree angle, as it often did, they were startled. What was only a matter of about five seconds seemed like eternity. The sheets flew up into the air and all Summer could see were huge breasts and butts, just skin flying everywhere. Ronnie had creeped up behind Summer, and caught as full of a view as Summer did. Apparently, she had not heard Summer say wait in the living room, and had followed behind her. Summer gasped and quickly closed the door, then hurried out of the apartment with Ronnie close behind her. Summer heard the apartment door slam as she headed quickly down the hallway. Leaving Ronnie in the hallway, she ran to the first exit door, then bolted down ten flights of stairs as fast as she could, trying not to trip or fall as she caught two steps at a time through teary eyes. Ordinarily she was deathly afraid of the exit. Nobody would go in there alone, especially not little girls, for fear of being raped or murdered. But, she was too shaken to care. She made it down safely and ran out of the building through the back entrance so that no one would see her crying. She went to the top parking lot and crouched behind the parked cars. She cried and cried there by herself for hours. She was angry, and confused about what she had seen, and she had no one to talk with about it. She just knew Ronnie would tell everyone and she would be embarrassed beyond repair, at school and outside in their neighborhood. She didn't know if her sisters would be mad at her for taking Ronnie in the house in the first place. She stood and peered over the edge of the top parking lot, which gave her a clear vantage point to the front of their building. Her sisters were not outside and she didn't know when they would be coming back. It was too late to go to Mrs. Smith's house. Mrs. Smith was an aide at her public school who had taken a liking to her, and happened to live in the building next to Summer's family. She would permit Summer to stop by, sit, talk, or even cry whenever she needed. She provided a safe haven for Summer to get things off of her chest. But, unfortunately, she could not go there now. She was on her own. She had to face this one all alone. She reasoned that she could not go back home to face Brenda and Mae. What would she say? What would they say to her? Was she in trouble? Would they think she was snooping? Did they even realize Ronnie was there? Was she supposed to understand all of this?

After about three hours, she got really scared about being up in the deserted parking lot alone and carefully made her way back down to the street-level. She snuck through the back of the building, and took the back stairwell up to the second floor, then walked down the hallway to the elevator banks. She wiped the tears from her face and tried to look normal, in case she ran into someone she knew. Luckily, no one was on the elevator. She rode alone up to the tenth floor. When she got off, no one was in the hallway, not even Ronnie. Summer hurried down the hall, quietly put her key in the door and entered the apartment. It was still dark, but this time it was completely quiet. Summer tip-toed toward the bedrooms, and noticed all the bedroom doors were closed. No lights were coming from underneath the doors of any of the rooms. Sabrina and Cheresse were still out somewhere, and Brenda and Mae appeared to be in a deep sleep. When she opened her bedroom door, Karla was snoring, oblivious to her arrival. Nobody had been out looking for her. Nobody was up waiting to talk to her about what had transpired. She changed into her pajamas, got into bed, and turned off the light. Then, she cried some more until she fell asleep.

The following morning when Summer woke up, Brenda and Mae were already gone. Everyone else was still asleep. Summer went into the kitchen, toasted two waffles, poured a glass of milk, then lost herself in the world of Bugs Bunny, trying to forget what she saw. Neither Brenda, nor Mae, nor Ronnie ever mentioned the incident.

Brenda: "Summer came to see me at the women's shelter in Manhattan when she was 23 years old, and told me this was one of the most painful times in her life," she trailed off.

> *Juwayriah: "And how did you respond?" she stopped writing notes and peered over at Brenda, who looked despondent.*
>
> *Brenda: "I told her I was really, really sorry. And I admitted I really didn't remember that day." "I was just so high all the time ... I don't remember a lot from those days," she said sadly.*

Busted!

Sometimes when people pray for things to happen, they have no idea what effect it will have on the rest of their lives. Brenda had prayed for many things in the time she had been with Mae. She prayed for God to turn back time and give her the strength to leave Mae at that bar. She prayed Mae would be dragged away from her by the police and thrown in prison for shoplifting. She prayed Silky would catch up to her and give her what she deserved. She even wished her dead, especially after Mae's threats of violence turned toward her daughters. Brenda knew she had to do something to get Mae away from her family, but what?

One day, they went to Bloomingdale's on Lexington Avenue in Manhattan for a flanking training session. While Brenda waited in the car with a guy Mae hired to drive, Mae went inside to collect the clothes she had stashed in a densely populated department in the store. She would then exit back out onto 59th Street and get into their awaiting car. The driver would then take them to a location on Long Island. From there, they would pay the guy and go back to Mae's apartment in Queens. That was the plan. When Mae went into the store, she gathered up four fur coats and shoved them into two shopping bags. This was before high end stores kept furs in more closely watched sections, and all clothing had sensors attached to them. Mae had made the mistake of putting the coats under a few of the tables while she went to get the others, and they were spotted, but not moved. When she went for them, the surveillance tape caught her. As she approached the door, security grabbed her and detained her and called the police.

When Mae failed to exit on 59th Street, Brenda and the guy knew something had gone wrong. Brenda followed the orders Mae had previously given, and instructed the guy to take off. He drove Brenda to Long Island, she paid him and she got on a train back to Manhattan. She then took the A train back home to Brooklyn and waited for the call from Rubenstein. He called seven hours later, just as Mae said he would confirming Mae had been busted for shoplifting. He told Brenda Mae would be released in a few days.

Mae was processed and taken by bus to Riker's Island Correctional Facility. Mae passed along instructions through Rubinstein for Brenda to take care of her business while she was being detained.

The instructions were as follows: Brenda was to go to the apartment in Queens and get some money Mae had stashed. Then she was to rent a car and go see a man named Bird who would give her even more money. All of the money was to be taken out to the wife of Reverend Odom in Long Island City. Brenda was then supposed to drive the Reverend's wife back to Mae's apartment, direct her to Mae's bedroom and then leave. She did as she was instructed.

Brenda took the opportunity, while Mae was out of her hair, to visit friends in the rental car and partied until 4 a.m. It was the only freedom she had from Mae in over two years, and she wanted to enjoy a few days of freedom, at Mae's expense. Because she was high, and it was closer than home, she drove back to Mae's apartment in an unusually heavy downpour of rain. She arrived safely and parked the car on the street. When she entered the apartment the Reverend's wife was gone. Brenda looked around the bedroom and in the corner by the bed she noticed a tiny black suitcase that hadn't been there earlier. When she flipped it open, there were tiny bottles of different colored liquids and a bottle with something hairy inside. She slammed it shut quickly and went to wash her hands. The Reverend's wife was a root worker and had been doing something at Mae's instruction. Brenda knew Mae practiced some kind of Santeria or Voodoo, but she had never done it in her presence. Mae believed that this practice had been protecting her from serving jail time, and from being harmed by others in her life. Brenda, who was raised in the church, did not believe in any of it, yet it made her nervous. She was exhausted from partying all night, and needed to get some rest. She fell asleep in Mae's bed.

That night she had terrible nightmares. In all the dreams, it was raining blood. Blood was all over the walls and blood was on her four daughters. She frantically kept trying to wipe the blood off of them, but instead it became heavier. She woke up in a pool of sweat, the sheets completely saturated. She immediately got dressed and left Mae's apartment as quickly as she could and drove home. She breathed a sigh of relief when she saw that all four of her daughters were safe and sound asleep in their beds. She changed her clothes and went to visit her friend Vera to tell her what happened. Vera agreed the Reverend's wife must have put roots on her, and that she needed to find somebody to get the roots off of her. Since Brenda had no money of her own, and she didn't know any root workers, she simply read her bible and prayed for God's protection over her children and herself. However, she never forgot the nightmares. Two days later, Mae was released from Riker's Island and back home. She laid low for a while, since things were too hot with her case pending.

Over the next two months, Brenda flanked alone. Mae sent Brenda to Bloomingdale's with specific instructions to get silk dresses, linen slacks and pocketbooks. Her best clients requested these items, and she had to produce. On Brenda's third trip she got busted. The security team grilled her for hours while the police were in route, and she was taken into custody. Brenda was taken to Central Booking and spent the night in the area referred to as the Tombs in lower Manhattan. Rubinstein came to see her immediately, just as Mae said he would. He posted bail for Brenda and she was released. She was placed on probation and assigned a probation officer.

Brenda was required to visit the probation officer in downtown Brooklyn, and it was one place where Mae could not go with her, or watch her movements. Brenda took these opportunities to hint around to her probation officer that she was in trouble. She couldn't tell the female officer directly, but she tried her best to tip her off about Mae. She would ask her why she was boosting and asking her why she would risk going to jail and losing her children. She played dumb, and kept quiet for the most part, telling the officer what she thought she wanted to hear. But, she kept hoping she would probe into her life and find something, or someone.

She thought about what she would do without Mae. At the time, the refrigerator was filled with good food. The house was furnished. She and her daughters always had beautiful designer clothes to wear. Brenda wasn't scrounging for pennies at a traditional job, or exhausted from working odd, long hours. She decided ambushing Mae was not the best play at the time.

One afternoon Mae burst into the apartment, locking all the locks on the front door behind her. She was pale and looked like she had just seen a ghost. She practically flew across the room past where Summer was watching television and slammed shut the vertical blinds on all the windows and the terrace door. Without saying a word, she ran into the bedroom, slammed the door and locked it. Clearly, she was terrified. There was dead silence in their room, and neither one of them came out for the rest of the night.

> *Brenda: "Mae had gotten comfortable and met up with one of her old connects in Jamaica, Queens. One of her old pimp's whores saw her and put the word out that she was in Jamaica. Luckily for Mae she always made good on favors and generously rewarded those who looked out for her. Someone gave her a head's up before Silky could arrive. He saw her hop into a taxi and got off a couple of shots just as the cab turned the corner. The driver said nothing after she gave him all the cash she was carrying at the time, $3,000 to drop her off at the LIRR Jamaica Station and keep his mouth shut" …… "It was no way to live," she said.*

Juwayriah: (Silently allowing Brenda to sit with that feeling, then) "Please, continue."

After that, Mae was more guarded and even more possessive. She was afraid to leave the house. She had Brenda run all her errands. Fear knocked her pride down just a peg, at least for a little while anyway. She seemed more accommodating, more calculated, more desperate, and less reckless. She kept peeking around corners and staying away from the windows in the apartment. She was terrified, and, for Brenda, it was satisfying to know she was not impenetrable. But, it didn't last long.

Losing it

Brenda and Mae would disappear for days. They'd be gone without explanation, then come home and sleep for half a day. On a warm day in May of 1980, Brenda called the payphone outside in front of their building. The home phone had been off for weeks, because Brenda didn't have the money to pay the phone bill and Mae didn't care because she was still hiding out. Usually, when Brenda needed to reach her daughters, she would call the pay phone hoping they were outside. Karla had been sitting on a bench talking with her friends, and Summer was in the townhouses playing with one of her friends. Any time the phone would ring, everyone in the general area could hear it. Most people who never received calls there would ignore it and continue with their conversations. But, if it were possible the call COULD be for you, your ears honed in and listened for your name. "KARLAAAA... phone!" Everyone would look over at the phone and see the receiver dangling. Summer poked her head up over the bushes and saw her sister running to the phone, then she went back to playing. It was part of the culture in the building, but it was also embarrassing, because everyone would assume your home phone was not working.

A few seconds later, Summer looked over at Karla in the distance and saw she was crying. She dropped everything and raced over to Karla to see what was wrong. She knew it was bad news, because Karla was now visibly sobbing in front of everyone, and she didn't seem to care. When Summer reached her sister, Karla simply handed her the phone and sat down on the knee-high brick wall close to the pay phone. Summer reluctantly said "Hello?" Brenda said softly "Hi, baby." Summer perked up, happy to hear her mother's voice "Hi, Mommy. Where are you?" She paused... then trying to sound upbeat "I'm in California." Suddenly, Summer was in a panic "What are you doing in California???" Brenda explained "Listen, I had to leave... and I won't be coming back." Summer was scared, and confused, and was listening for more. She was trying to digest it. Did she hear correctly? What did she mean? Mothers can't just go to California like that. She didn't understand. Did she mean for a while? Did she mean forever? What was she talking about? Summer was trying to process it all in the few seconds she had to talk with her mother. Her 8th grade graduation was in two weeks, and Brenda had promised to buy her a class ring, a graduation dress, give her the money for her cap and gown, and a pretty pair of shoes! She promised! She had never missed any of her sisters' graduations. How could she miss HERS?! She cried "What about MY graduation?!" Brenda cried too, then said weakly, "I know. I know. I'm so sorry baby, I'm sorry I can't be there." She paused, as if she wanted to say more, but didn't. "I just can't" she rushed the words. "I can't explain right now. But, I love you so much. I'm so sorry." Summer could hear her crying now on the other end, too. Summer was straining to hear anything in the background that would help answer all of the questions she had, but she heard nothing, just sniffles. Both girls and their mother were all bawling their eyes out now. None of them knew what to do. Things had never gotten this bad before. Why was this happening? There were so many questions, and no time for answers. Then Summer heard Mae in the background "COME ON, BRENDA!" Brenda blubbered the words, "Okay, I have to go now, baby. I love you." All Summer could say was "I love you, too." And with that she hung up. She looked at Karla, and Karla looked back at her. They were too afraid to look over at the benches where they knew people would be staring at them.

They went upstairs to tell Cheresse what happened. They were hoping she would be able to tell them what they were supposed to do next. As a freshman trying to navigate her first year in college, this was the last thing Cheresse needed to hear. She looked more pissed off than sad like the other girls. Her face turned red with anger. She grabbed her house keys, told them to stay there in the apartment, and left. She went down to Cynthia's house to tell her what had happened. Then she used Cynthia's phone to call Kate and Jimmy. Kate drove from Queens, Jimmy made his way through traffic from the Bronx, and Sabrina took the A train to the other end of Brooklyn to be with her sisters.

It had been over a year since Sabrina had been in the apartment, and she felt uneasy being there. She sat on the couch, and looked around the apartment, feeling a wave of emotions. She became an adult in this room… watching her mother be a child, and her mother watching her become a woman. She fought for her independence here, stood her ground here, and broke free from this place where her sisters were still trapped, until today.

They all discussed the situation. Cheresse would have to quit school and get a full-time job. Sabrina had been working full-time already, and was also attending college. Cynthia had arranged for them to keep the apartment under the section 8 housing plan, which was available for low-income families. Since Karla and Summer were still minors, they had to have a legal guardian caring for them. They just assumed they would either stay in the apartment with Sabrina and Cheresse, or they would go back to Queens to live with Kate and Dave.

Summer was about to begin her freshman year studying cosmetology at Mabel Dean Bacon Vocational High School in Manhattan, and was thinking about how her commute would be traveling all the way from Queens to Manhattan. Karla, who was now 17, felt she was almost legal and figured she would just stay in the apartment, too. She was supposed to be finishing up high school that year. She and Karla never even considered that their father would take legal custody of them, but that is exactly what he did. Jimmy thought about his father looking down at his two sons on a cold day in Harlem, name tags tied around their coat buttons, and leaving them in the hands of strangers. His daughters were not babies, like he and his brother were then, but for the next few years he would figure out a way to take care of them.

He considered the situation. He would have to break the news to Sophia that these children, who he has never had to raise during their entire marriage, would now have to live with them. He had no choice. As could be expected under the circumstances, it did not go well. For one, they had been living in the two-bedroom ground floor apartment in her parent's brownstone in the Bronx. Her parents lived on the first floor, and her sister lived on the top floor with her family. There was no room for two more people. Jimmy had been working for the New York City

Department of Sanitation, and did have his salary and benefits. But, he had joint financial obligations with his wife, which would make it very difficult to also now care for two children financially. He alone would have to provide for his daughters. It was going to be tough, but he knew he had to figure out a way. He could not let someone else raise his daughters, he simply could not do that to his girls. He would somehow find a happy medium.

Jimmy, Sabrina and Cheresse had decided, along with Kate's blessing, that the two minors would both go live with Jimmy. Jimmy went to court, filed for custody, and was quickly granted the right to raise his daughters since Brenda did not show up to contest. Karla and Summer were shocked, scared and furious. They didn't know anything about the Bronx. They had only heard horror stories about how bad and riddled with crime the Bronx was. Also, they were afraid to go live with their father. They didn't really know him anymore, not on a day-to-day basis. They had no idea what to expect. The Bronx was only a few boroughs away, but for Karla and Summer, it felt like a foreign land. Brooklyn felt safe, the Bronx did not. The media had painted such a bleak picture of the Bronx in the 80's, and it left the girls afraid and paranoid. There was always someone on the news being robbed, stabbed or raped in the Bronx. But, that wasn't the worst part of going to the

Bronx. More than anything, they would really miss their Brooklyn friends.

Sophia had never been much of a stepmother to Jimmy's daughters. They didn't know what to think or how to feel about her, or their dad, or anything that was happening really. Sophia seemed averse to his children and appeared to make herself scarce most of the time on the rare occasions they would visit his home. She fussed around the house uncomfortably, asking sweetly "Would you like some iced tea? A piece of cake?" It was hospitable, an offer that would be extended to any guest in her home, it seemed. It wasn't warm or familial, in that "my home is your home" kind of way. Not a welcome exchange that a loving stepmom and stepdaughters would have with one another.

When Jimmy brought Karla and Summer to a 6-story, walk-up apartment building at 149 West 179th Street, two blocks from Bronx Community College, they were confused. He used a key to a mostly empty apartment on the 4th floor and announced this was their new home. The building was directly around the corner from Sophia's parent's home. From the living room window the girls could scream out "Daddy" and he could either stick his head out of the back window and talk up to them, or he could walk out of the side door to the back of the house and look up to find out what his daughters needed. They did not have a telephone in the apartment to call anyone in the event of an emergency. A telephone was an expense that could not be justified in Jimmy's budget at the time. Karla dropped out of high school and worked the night shift at Burger King to help Jimmy pay the rent. It was the only way he could make it work, and it was still a struggle. While Karla worked at night, 14-year-old Summer was home alone, with all the windows and doors locked, and the blinds pulled down. The view from their bedroom windows was the side of a brick house, and was framed by a fire-escape. Summer spent many terrified nights, wide-eyed in the quiet darkness, listening for anyone perched on the fire-escape, watching her sleep, waiting for the right moment to break in and rape or kill her. She'd had to force herself to go to sleep, so she wouldn't be exhausted in school. The worst part in all the transition was that Shep could not go with Summer to the Bronx. Summer's heart had been completely torn out when she was forced to give him away. First, she lost her mother, now she had lost her best friend.

Jimmy found an old man on Shepherd Avenue in Brooklyn, close to their apartment in East New York, who had agreed to take Shep. He owned a salvage yard and needed a guard dog. Since Jimmy was giving him away for free, the man was skeptical and wanted to take a look at him. Summer was told to gather up all of Shep's things, and she, Jimmy,

Karla and Cheresse drove in Jimmy's car over to the salvage yard. When

they pulled up, the man came out of his house, which was adjacent to the

junkyard. The house was run down and filthy looking from the outside.

The yard was very greasy with old broken-down cars and car parts, and

there was no place really for a dog to run around. There was another dog

in the yard chained to the side of the metal fence who was in desperate

need of a bath. Summer knew right away that the old man would not

treat Shep with love. Shep was a house dog, not used to being outside

with other dogs, especially dirty ones. The man was really old and mean

looking. She knew he was going to tie Shep to the gate just like the other

dog. He was going to feed him scraps (if he fed him at all) and never

wash him. Summer cried and begged her father to keep Shep He said

there was no way she could. It tore her heart into a thousand pieces to

leave him there, but she had no choice. At the time, Summer felt more

broken up about losing Shep than she did about losing her mother to

Mae. She had come to know her mother as absent, and unpredictable.

But, Shep was loyal, and constant, and trustworthy. She hugged him

tightly around his neck, warm tears buried inside his freshly bathed,

herbal scented patches of soft, salt and pepper hair. His wet tongue hanging to one side of his mouth on that hot, sticky June day. With his heavy panting in her right ear and both of their hearts beating fast, she said goodbye to her special friend. She hated her mother more than ever...

After a few months, Karla and Summer had settled into their new home and even made a few friends. They were permitted to be outside until dark, then back in the apartment, doors locked. Jimmy would stop by most days to ensure they had the basic food groups in the refrigerator, and to reassure himself there was no funny business going on in the way of boys or drugs, etc. Summer had become friends with a classmate named Amanda Flood, who happened to live a few blocks away in a 13-story tan brick building on Sedgwick Avenue. She was an only child living with a single mom, who made a good living as a nurse. Summer was happy to have a travel buddy to and from school in Manhattan, and loved the solace of visiting a friend her age during such a scary time.

A little after midnight, one day while Karla was at work, Summer was awakened by a sudden, sharp pain in her lower abdomen. She didn't move at first, waiting to see if it would go away. Another sharp pain came. She wrapped both arms around her belly and curled into a ball under the covers in the dark. She wondered what she had eaten that could be making her stomach hurt this way. Under the covers she felt her underwear wet and warm. "Freak!" she thought to herself, "peed in the bed, again." She didn't want to get up, wash, change clothes, change sheets, scrub the mattress, then sleep on the edge until morning while it dried. She was too sleepy. Another sharp pain, harder this time. She felt her underwear to determine whether it could wait until morning. Her underwear felt wet and warm, not cold like it would if she had urinated. She got up, feeling her way to the bathroom in the darkness. She sat down on the toilet, pulled down her underwear and waited for her bowels to give her some relief. Nothing came, except pain. She could see the large dark spot in the cotton part of her underwear where it should have been white, and became frightened. She got up and turned on the light. When she looked down, she saw blood, lots of it, and panicked. Her heart raced, and she began to cry. She had finally gotten her period. What was she supposed to do? She took off the underwear and threw them into the sink, running warm water over them. She had seen girls at school take large wads of toilet paper and shove it into their underwear, so she did that. She pushed the tissue up into her vagina a little, as if to stop a bloody nose, and walked cowboy-style back to her bedroom. She took a clean pair of underwear from the top drawer of the little four-drawer cardboard dresser Jimmy had bought from the hardware store, and pulled them up over the bunched wad of paper.

It was 2am. She didn't have a phone to call her father, or anyone else. She wasn't about to scream out of the window for Jimmy at this hour. And what would she say if he came to the window, or came around the corner, up four flights and standing in front of her at this hour asking "What's wrong??" She sobbed into her pillow. She would have to wait until 7am for Karla to get home.

In August of 1981, Karla turned 18 and claimed her independence from Jimmy. She called Sabrina and Cheresse and asked if she could move back to Brooklyn and into her old bedroom. They agreed. That left the question "What to do with Summer?" Jimmy was able to make it work out with Karla there, but now he had no choice.

Jimmy cleared out the apartment, and Summer moved in with her father and Sophia on the 1st floor of Sophia's parents' brownstone on Loring Place. Sophia's parents had both since passed away, leaving Sophia's sister's family on the top floor and a tenant in the ground floor apartment where Sophia and Jimmy had lived years earlier.

A winding brick staircase from the street led up to the 1st floor entrance of the house. The foyer area opened up into a wide, carpeted living room on the right, then continued through a dining room, and into a warm, bright sunroom filled with enough green plants to make any horticulturist envious. It was a room someone obviously loved.

From the foyer, you could see straight to the back of the apartment, looking through the living room, kitchen, bathroom, and to a back, spare bedroom, railroad house style. The house smelled clean, like pledge and Pine Sol, and everything had its place. The décor in the house was pretty much unchanged from the last time Summer had been there years earlier. Lots of dark wood furniture, floral patterns accenting the décor, and brown paneling on the walls. There were also lots of photos of Sophia's happy family, Sophia and Jimmy with Sophia's cousins and friends on vacation at Disney, joyous holiday gatherings, and just enough photos to fit on one hand sprinkled in of Jimmy's children to acknowledge they existed. Those photos were intermingled into those white, matted multi-photo picture frames with squares and circles for headshots. It was a clear microcosm of Jimmy's life without his girls.

Sophia's mother had passed away first, then a few years after, her Dad. In his final years, Sophia was his primary caregiver until he eventually died in the first room on the right, down the hallway directly past the kitchen. This is would be Summer's room for the next year.

The room showed no signs of life, warmth or color. It actually felt like a tomb. Queen sized mahogany bed with a high headboard and footboard, old fashioned white comforter, two pillows with white pillowcases. Above the headboard high on the otherwise bare, gray wall a dark wooden statue of Jesus on the cross. Opposite the bed was an empty dresser with a huge mahogany framed mirror, making it impossible to see anything else but the Son of God from the last moment you close your eyes at night to the first thing you see upon opening your eyes in the morning. There was a matching dark mahogany chest of drawers in the corner, an empty closet and a white draped window facing the alley separating Sophia's house from the house next door. There was nothing in the room that would make a 15-year-old girl feel welcome. No flowers, no plants, no bright colors (no colors at all), no frilly bedspread, and definitely no television.

Summer didn't want to sit on the bed, let alone sleep in it. She did not want to unpack her clothes. She didn't want to put them in any of the drawers. She didn't want to hang any of her clothes up in there. How was she going to sleep here? She went to the bathroom and sobbed in silence. She was more furious than ever at Brenda, and Jimmy. She just wanted to go back to Brooklyn.

The house was eerily silent the first night. Sophia had prepared a meal and dished out two plates for Jimmy and Summer, placing them at the kitchen table. She then disappeared into her bedroom and closed the door for the night. Admittedly, Summer was grateful for a warm plate of Spanish food (Arroz con Pollo), hot buttered bread, and cup of homemade lemonade. Sophia was a really good cook and baker. Summer didn't want to love the food so much, but she hadn't had a home cooked meal since she was last at Kate's house (almost a year earlier). She resented that it was so delicious. The enticing, savory scent of Sazon and Sofrito that filled the house earlier had manifested into this fragrant meal before her. The tender, juicy chicken and fluffy yellow rice seemed to dissolve in her mouth and warmed her belly. She wanted to believe it was Sophia's way of expressing love to a girl who had just lost her mother. But, aside from the great meal, she felt unwelcome, like she had stolen that small portion of food lovingly prepared and intended for an actual loved one.

Jimmy and Summer did not speak over dinner, except to say 'Goodnight' to one another. Summer was grateful the next day was not a school day, and she could collect her thoughts and feelings. Living together was not easy for Jimmy, Sophia or Summer. Jimmy was working, had to manage his wife's feelings, being a new full-time father, and managing his teenage daughter's emotions. To stay out of the house as much as possible, Summer asked to visit Amanda quite often. Jimmy was wary of everyone, people in the neighborhood hung out in the street too much, people who smoked drugs and drank on the block, people who were too loud, boys who might try to 'sniff around' young girls, and he was even wary of Amanda. He met Amanda just once. He thought she was 'fast' and was too into boys. He thought she would be a bad influence for Summer. He also knew Amanda's mother was single and worked a lot, leaving Amanda without much supervision. Summer, of course, LOVED this and tried to visit Amanda as much as possible. Amanda's apartment always had good food and snacks to eat. Summer was always grateful for the tasty food Sophia made, but she was rarely full afterwards. Sophia would make the plates, then quickly pack up the food, storing it in the refrigerator before she could ask for more. So, she sometimes went to bed hungry.

Amanda didn't have that problem. Her mother always made sure she had money for school, and since she worked a lot there was always good food in the fridge and cabinets. Amanda wore the flyest bomber jackets with fur, fresh Jordache jeans, gold 'Amanda' name chain, and crisp shell-top Adidas. When her mother was not working, she relaxed and busied herself on the phone, cleaned the house or watched television, leaving us to play hip hop music in Amanda's bedroom or walk to the store. Summer envied Amanda for having a cool, career-driven mother who seemed normal. Her whole life seemed normal to Summer. Her

life was a mess as far as she was concerned, and she did her best to avoid

living it. She had to get out of the Bronx.

By early 1983, Summer had convinced her sisters to let her return to

Brooklyn, to stay in the apartment they all shared years earlier.

> *Juwayriah: How do you feel about the part you've played in*
> *all of these things you've shared Brenda? It's a lot to accept and*
> *manage.*
>
> *Brenda: (Pause) Yes, it's a terrible burden. I will carry it*
> *always. I spent lots of time going over and over in my head*
> *about what I could have done differently. But, back then, I*
> *honestly didn't think I had choices.*
>
> *Juwayriah: There is always a choice.*

Brenda recounted that after Mae had come home in a panic, she told

her she had to run away from her old pimp, that he had taken shots at

her, and that he was close on her trail. She said she had to get out of

town. Brenda believed her, and suggested she go alone. Mae said she

was too scared to be out there on her own, and insisted Brenda go, too.

She became enraged, calling her ungrateful and began threatening her.

Brenda tried to reason with her "I can't just leave my kids." Mae lit a

cigarette, then blew her smoke in Brenda's face, "If you don't go with

me something unfortunate could happen to your kids." She said if

Brenda stayed behind the pimp would kill her and her daughters. But, if

they left now he would hear that she left town and he won't be looking

for her at Brenda's place. Brenda knew the pimp was a bad man, and

could actually be capable of finding them and hurting her daughters. Or

worse than that, he could try to recruit her daughters! And she didn't

want that man anywhere near them. So, she felt she had no choice but

to go with her and leave her daughters behind, for their own safety.

Road Dirt & Regret

They had packed a few bags and hopped on a Greyhound bus headed for Sacramento, California. Brenda had never been to California before. Hell, she had never even been outside of New York, except to take trips with Kate to visit family and friends in New Jersey, Pennsylvania and Delaware. This would be a real adventure, she told herself.

She was relieved Mae had fallen off to sleep, so she could be alone with her thoughts. Out of the bus window she watched New York disappear, and everything else that had been her life up until that point. She turned her head toward the window as far as she could without stirring Mae, who's head and long red wig were propped up on Brenda's shoulder. It was hot and musty on the bus and Brenda was sweating and uncomfortable. She gently slid her arm away from Mae, so she could turn her whole body sideways toward the window. She silently let the tears fall. She was grateful that it was dark on the bus, and that most everyone was asleep with Mae.

She wanted to bolt off the bus, and go back home, but then what? Mae would just come right back for her. No, it was better this way. She would somehow find a way to get away from Mae, but she needed to do this. She had to get Mae far away from her daughters. This was the only way she could think of to make sure her daughters would be ok.

She reasoned they would have a better chance of making it without her. The truth was, they were already taking care of themselves, and had been since Mae moved in. She admitted to herself that she had barely been there for them as it was. She almost patted herself on the back for the great job she had done with preparing them to be self-sufficient. Even Summer had become independent and was about to graduate from junior high school. She had been getting herself up and dressed for school since fourth grade. She made her own meals and lunch, simple stuff like sandwiches and she believed she had seen her cook eggs, but she couldn't recall for sure. Or was she thinking of Karla? Either way, she knew Summer would be ok. She thought of the dog. Summer would certainly take care of the dog, she had already been doing that since Mae brought the dog home. Brenda smiled for a moment. Then she was sad again, remembering she had broken many promises, especially not buying Summer a graduation dress. Kate had always made sure she was perfect for every event in her life as a child. She never had to worry about such things. But, what could she say? She could only apologize, and pray one day she would understand that. Her timing sure was poor though, she thought. It was too painful to relive, so she let her mind go blank. She could really use a joint right now, she thought. The signs said they were passing through Ohio. Brenda dozed off.

The bus stopped somewhere in Indiana. Mae shook Brenda awake, and told her they were getting off the bus to stretch their legs and get something to eat. It wasn't an invitation as much as it was an order. Brenda pulled herself up from the seat, feeling like she had been dragged under the bus for the past twelve hours. She followed Mae into the rest stop building, where Mae paid for the order she placed for them, sunny side up eggs, bacon, and a short stack of pancakes, with a side of fresh squeezed orange juice. Mae always ordered sunny side up eggs, disregarding the fact that Brenda hated her eggs that way. When the eggs arrived at the table, Brenda ate the eggs in silence. "What the hell is wrong with YOU?" Mae said, as if she didn't know. "I know you're worried about the girls, but they gonna be fine," she used her fork as her finger to make her point toward Brenda's face. She continued, "That's why they got a Daddy." Mae left that hanging in the air for a few minutes giving Brenda time to think about this and see her point. "It's about time he did *something* for them anyway, he's wayyy overdue and you know it," she said as she cut and took a bite of her eggs. Brenda didn't speak.

She was staring out of the window, watching weary travelers eager to get off of the buses for a chance to stretch, or eagerly board buses to hurry their journeys along. As she turned back to Mae and watched her eat, nothing ruining her appetite. It always annoyed Brenda how Mae took the runny, sunny eggs and sat them on top of the buttered toast, then slurped them up, like she had no home training. Kate would be mortified if she could see this. If Brenda ever ate her food like that growing up, Kate would have her head. Kate... despite everything they had been through over the years, she truly loved her Mom. Kate had been the only mom she had ever known, and there had never been so much distance between them.

Brenda picked up her fork and began to eat, to avoid having to fight with Mae in the busy restaurant about how she was 'wasting her money' by not eating the food she so graciously bought for her. Her thoughts trailed off as Mae rattled on about what they were going to do once they reached California.

Kate was going to be mad as hell at her for running off and leaving her kids. She and Dave had already told her she was a disappointment. They didn't understand what she was going through. They couldn't understand that she needed Mae to help her out with taking care of things. How else was she supposed to get money to feed them, clothe them, pay for dancing school and other activities? Well, actually, she had to be honest with herself that Kate had funded most of the girls' activities, including years of dance lessons, school pictures, and trips over the years. It had been nearly eight months since she talked to Kate, who called to talk to the girls to see how they were doing. Brenda was in the middle of a heated fight with Mae, over her undercharging one of Mae's clients for two silk blouses and a Diane Von Furstenburg dress. She answered the phone angrily "HELLO!" Kate responded "Brenda?" Brenda softened her tone, and held her hand up to Mae so she wouldn't continue her rant, "Hi, Ma, how are you? How's Dad?" Pause. "He's good. We were wondering how the girls were. We haven't seen them in a long while. Is everything ok?" Trying to sound upbeat and happy, normal, "Yes, everything is fine. Cheresse started college, she likes it a lot so far." Brenda had no idea whether Cheresse liked college, nor did she know how she was managing with classes. She just thought it sounded good, and would be what Kate wanted to hear. "Are the girls around, can I speak to them?" She was disappointed Kate hadn't asked how she was. "Um, no, they're not around right now. But, I can have them call you when they get back home," she said, trying to sound upbeat. It was like she was talking to a stranger, or a bill collector. Kate waited, likely trying to hear if anything was going on in the background. Mae was sitting on the bed, watching Brenda like a hawk, listening to her voice rise and fall as she spoke with Kate. She couldn't stand how Brenda backed down from her mother, and begged for her to love her and approve of her. Brenda was weak in her mind, and she told her many times that she shouldn't "kiss Kate's ass" the way she did. Mae told her she didn't need Kate judging her and making her feel like she wasn't shit all the time. Brenda did feel that Kate could have been a bit more understanding, and show her a little more compassion than she did. And she thought Dave could have given her a break when she called to see how he was, to tell him she loved and missed him. But, he refused to reciprocate. He and Kate both lectured her, and tried to tell her how to live her life. They absolutely despised Mae, and told her each chance they got. Once Brenda screamed at them and told them to "Mind their own damn business", they backed off. She couldn't believe she had spoken to them in such a way, as she never had before in her life. They couldn't know she had been smoking weed and sniffing coke for two days straight. She wasn't herself, she was sure they could see that and would try to understand she was 'in a bad way.'

After that, Kate and Dave just stopped calling. Kate said she was 'giving her over to the Lord' and Dave said nothing. His silence was louder than any words he could have said to her, and it hurt her deeply.

When they would call, they only asked about the girls. Brenda truly

regretted disappointing them the way she had. They had done so much

for her, more than anyone else had in her life. More than Alice, or Dill,

and especially her real daddy, whose identity she was still unsure of. She

had always suspected Dill was not her real father, but she hadn't had any

proof until she was 16 years old.

She was pregnant and had been upstairs folding a freshly laundered batch of clothes Kate had taken out of the dryer, when her Aunt Cilla and Uncle Gerald came for a visit. Aunt Cilla was quite a drinker, her choice of poison being whiskey, and at any time of the day or night. She arrived a bit sloshy, but with loud, happy greetings and pleasantries thrown around the room, all in one fell swoop. Brenda could hear the almost ritualistic sound of her walking across the living room floor straight to the spirits cart in the corner of the den, then the familiar sound of crystal clanking against the glass tray where all the bottles rested. She would be seated in her favorite chair in the den with her drink in her hand within three minutes easy. Brenda smiles to herself, finding comfort somehow in the routine of it all. After a few moments, she could hear Uncle Gerald's voice go an octave higher than when he had arrived. "Kate, I know he's your brother, but he ain't never been any good, not to her, and he ain't never been good to Brenda." Hearing her name perked up her ears a notch. She tip-toed closer to the doorway of the middle bedroom, to position herself near the floor vents that lead downstairs in the living room. "Shhh" she heard Kate whisper. Aunt Cilla sloshed her words laced with indignation only she could deliver, "He's not her Daddy anyway, everybody know it, right Kate?" Then there was silence. Brenda held her breath at this confirmation. She didn't move for fear they would hear her moving across the floorboards. A few seconds later, the conversation turned to their favorite topic, politics. From that moment forward, Brenda had fantasized about who her real dad was and where he was. She wondered if he even knew she existed. She couldn't ask Kate about it, because she would know she was snooping. But, that was the first time she had hope that there was a father for her out there somewhere that might love her, and be thinking of her, maybe even missing her.

Reflections

Back on the bus and heading toward Indiana, she promised herself she was going to get her life together. She just had to figure out a plan. She would get back to New York, and she would beg her daughters' forgiveness. And, maybe, in time, her mom and dad would understand why she had to leave. They had been the only parents she'd known, and they told her on many occasions since she and Jimmy divorced that they were disappointed in her. She cried some more, as they passed through Illinois.

Brenda had lots of questions going around in her mind during the bus ride. What would her girls do now that she was gone? How would they pay the rent? How would they eat? Who would make sure Karla and Summer go to school, and do their homework, and who would protect them from the bad men in the streets? She knew there were plenty out there, because many of them were Mae's clients and customers. Mae had introduced her to lots of drug dealers and numbers men, just about anyone who was willing to run a scheme. She loved any man who was gullible enough, or greedy enough to help her pull off her schemes.

Brenda wanted these people to stay far away from her daughters. They were good girls. She had always said so.

She wasn't worried so much for Cheresse. She was very street savvy, and no nonsense. Most people didn't understand her, thought she was mean or stuck up. But, she knew better. Cheresse was kind and sweet at heart, but she didn't let people get close to her, not until she could trust them. And she noticed that group included her sisters, and possibly one other friend in the neighborhood, Dana. They had spent lots of time together during high school years, going to movies together, going to parties together and dressing alike, same red pants, same white button-down shirt, same red espadrilles. It was nice to see her find someone she could get close to, someone she could call a friend. She did have a boyfriend who was 'sniffing around.' Brenda knew for a fact he was a criminal, but she wasn't sure which kind exactly (drugs, guns, girls). He was quite a playboy, sharp dresser, very popular, and handsome. Nevertheless, Brenda knew that Cheresse was no slouch and could handle herself, even with that boyfriend. She was strong, the strongest in her mind. She thought of her light-skinned, hazel-eyed, almond-shaped face now. She had a beautiful smile, and brains, too. Yes, she would be ok.

Sabrina was already taking care of herself, and becoming more of a woman every day. Brenda could admit to herself that things didn't end on a good note with the two of them, and she did regret not speaking to Sabrina after she moved out. It was just too hard with Mae always in her ear, bad-mouthing her daughters.

Brenda really respected Sabrina. She was outspoken, feisty, sweet, smart, and beautiful. She was ALL of the things Brenda wasn't. She greatly admired her daughter because of it. Even though she hadn't planned the fight, she couldn't have hoped for a better outcome. She couldn't recall every detail. At the time, she was too high. But, she remembered the terrible fight. She wanted to jump up and help them, but her legs wouldn't move. Her brain wouldn't start, her eyes felt heavy and she felt paralyzed. She kept screaming at herself in her own head "GET UP, GET HER," but she wasn't sure why she was saying it and exactly WHO she should be 'getting.' When she finally broke through whatever was holding her back, Sabrina's face was bleeding and her heart leaped out of her chest. She saw Sabrina screaming in her face, but she couldn't hear what she was saying. Sabrina left the room, and she saw Mae on the floor looking like she had been in a barroom brawl. She was stunned to see Mae on the floor. She wanted to run after Sabrina, but her feet wouldn't budge. Then Kate came and lost her mind on them, and she didn't know what to do. She looked for Sabrina, and wanted to bring her back and talk to her, but then things spiraled way out of control and before she knew it Sabrina had moved out! She knew Cynthia could have reported her to the police, child protective services or anyone, with her connections in local government. Who knows how much Sabrina had shared with her about what was going on? So, she decided not to say anything. She had already said too much that could have made Cynthia come after her.

She didn't want it to happen that way, but she was glad Sabrina was away from Mae. She had already been making plans to bring Sabrina and Cheresse into her boosting schemes. She kept saying they were the 'right age' to help make money for the family. Well, Brenda patted herself on the back, SHE used her smarts to get Mae away from them.

Summer was still so tiny, smaller and 'less developed' than the other girls her age. She thought of her brown, button face, and pony-tailed hair. She was in junior high now. She couldn't believe her baby was graduating from 8th grade already. She beamed with pride. Then, just as fast, a pain in her heart as she remembered she would miss her graduation. She had never missed a graduation before, not for any of them. No matter what was going on in her life, she could always say she was there for all of their milestones. Her sisters would take care of her, make sure she does the right thing, and stays out of trouble. They always had! She would make it up to Summer, one day, she thought.

She worried most for Karla. She was more like Brenda than the other three. She was a pretty, brown-skinned girl with a sweet, welcoming smile, and great sense of humor. Everybody loved to hang around her, because she was kind, gentle, and sweet. Like Brenda though, she was too trusting of others, and quite rebellious. She didn't do as well in school as the others, and Brenda believed she turned to her personality to get her by. Benda always related to that part of Karla's personality. She wanted to save her from all the pitfalls she had fallen into when she was her age, boyfriend too early, teen pregnancy, staying away from drugs. But, she just didn't make the time for her. Brenda regretted this most of all, because she could relate to her best. And she was the only one who understood Karla, and didn't protect her. Now she had left her, and her heart felt broken.

She was crying out loud now, searching for tissue in her pocket. Mae stopped in the middle of telling Brenda her story about her man Jeffrey in San Francisco who was waiting for them, saw Brenda's tears and said loud enough for a few rows in all directions to hear "What the FUCK you sittin' here CRYING about??? I ain't havin' no CRYIN' around me 24/7!" Passengers were turning around and craning their necks to see what the commotion was. Mae leaned her head into the aisle and smiled at them to let them know everything was ok. They went back to sleeping, snacking, reading, listening to walkmans, or looking out of the window. Trying to stay calm and calm Brenda down too, "Brenda, you gotta stop this shit now. We movin' on now, it's done. They gonna be ok, I know it." "They smart, and resourceful, AND they pretty. They got a lot goin' for em. They gonna be ok without us." Brenda shot her a look. "US??" she thought. 'Oh, NOW she wanted to admit her girls were smart and resourceful?' A minute ago they were fast whores, bitches and stupid.

Brenda mustered a half-smile, while she wiped the tears from her face, and said just softly enough "I know, you're right."

She reassured herself 'I love my girls, and they love me.' At least she believed they still would, even after all of this.   They had a special connection that mothers and daughters have, right? She had to believe that somewhere in their hearts, they would still love her, still know they had a mother that loves THEM. It was all she had.

She looked out of the window as they passed through farm country. It was nighttime again. Nearly pitch-black outside except for the few tall streetlights along the deserted back road. She wondered where they were now.

Deliverance

They had no money by the time they got to California, and they didn't know anyone there. People weren't allowed to walk the streets all night in Sacramento then, so the first few nights they slept in an alleyway behind a restaurant and scrounged in the garbage bins for food. But, Mae wasn't going to have much of that.

Mae had convinced Brenda to call Dill to ask for money. She reasoned he had never done anything for her during her whole life, and it was the LEAST he could do to wire her a couple of hundred dollars to get on her feet again. Brenda knew it was a bad idea, but Mae promised they would go get high afterwards. So, she went out to the pay phone on the corner and dialed Dill and Alice's home number. She waited nervously for someone to answer, once, twice. Dill answered on the third ring. "Hello?" As pleasant as could be. His familiar, Pennsylvanian Southern-ish accent sounding more like 'yalluh' than a greeting. She almost hung up, but forced out "Hi Dad, it-it's Brenda." Pause. Oh, hello Brenda, how are you doing?" It was an uneasy question, and she immediately lied "I'm doing pretty well. Out here in California visiting a friend." She kept going, fearing she'd lose her nerve, "I was just wondering if you could loan me a couple of hundred dollars? I lost my wallet, and I'm trying to get back to New York as soon as possible!" She tried to sound upbeat like asking for money from her loving father was natural. She continued, "I tried to call Marilyn a few times in Berkeley, but she hasn't been home." She wanted to let him know she had thought of that, and had at least been resourceful enough to exhaust her options before calling him. She thought it made her seem more responsible. He was silent. She could hear the familiar sound of Monty Hall telling someone they had won a new car. What was only a few seconds felt like an eternity. Dill replied "Well... you know things are tight over here...". She didn't let him continue, letting both of them off the hook "That's ok" she said hurriedly. "I'll figure it out. Thanks anyway. I'll talk to you soon" she lied, then hung up the phone. She immediately regretted calling. She cried a river of tears in that closed phone booth. She wanted so badly for him to just give her some sign he was her father, that she was at least his daughter. How could he feel absolutely nothing? She couldn't dwell on it now. She had to go back and tell Mae Dill said no. She'd call him a "Low life Nigga" like she always did. Brenda didn't want to hear any of Mae's shit. Right now, she just wanted to get high.

A couple of boosting jobs and a few good customers got them back on their feet and into some nice hotel suites for a while. They watched a lot of television and ate peanuts when they couldn't be out on the street. Brenda acquired a job as cab driver for a little extra cash, and Mae headed over to the department stores. They were doing okay for close to 8 months. But, soon the police were hot on Mae's trail and they had to leave Sacramento. They spent the next 6 months in Oakland then migrated to Berkeley, California. They weren't in Berkeley long before Mae spotted a poster with her face on it at a major department store, and decided it wasn't worth the risk. She needed to move on. So, they left California and headed South. They got on a bus and headed to Sheltsburg, Mae's home town. Brenda tried to call the payphone back in Brooklyn a few times, the girls were never outside. She couldn't know that Karla and Summer were now living in the Bronx, and her two eldest daughters were working. She had become totally disconnected from everyone and everything she had ever known.

Mae's family didn't want anything to do with her either. She had phoned her mother while in Berkeley, and each time Mae would spend most of the call listening to her mother berate her. She called her a filthy whore, and sometimes refused her calls. She only accepted Mae's calls when money was running low for her son. If Mae refused to send money, her mother would curse her out "GO TO HELL WHERE YOU BELONG, WHORE!" She would guilt Mae by telling her that her son (16-years-old then) hated her, too. She would become furious and hang up, then she would wire one, two, three thousand dollars to her mother. It was a hate-hate relationship.

When they arrived by taxi at her mother's house Mae told Brenda to stay in the car. She stepped out with a very sharp, tailor made, fitted pink church skirt suit, black snake skin pumps, a black Jackie-O pill-box hat with pink lace and pearls around the edge, a square pink purse with black piping, respectable short black wig, and a flawless made up face. She was carrying a fat brown envelope in her other hand. She rang the doorbell. A woman answered the door, neatly dressed but not fashionable. She was a handsome-looking, light-skinned woman with straight shiny red hair pulled back into a neat ponytail. She was only taller than Mae by a quarter inch. She did not look happy to see Mae at all. Brenda could see the woman over Mae's shoulder leaning on the door jam, glaring at Mae and twisting her lips to the side in disgust. Brenda could only imagine what hateful and hurtful things she must have been saying to Mae, but Mae's back was tall and strong from behind. She did not seem to be backing down with whatever it was she was saying to the woman. Mae held up the envelope in her right hand, and the woman stood up straight. The woman looked over Mae's shoulder and saw Brenda in the car. Brenda knew better than to wave or smile. She sat back so that the woman could not see her. When Brenda leaned up a minute later, she saw Mae turn around and begin to walk toward the cab. She flung the brown envelope over her shoulder, and did not look back. The woman calmly walked down the two porch steps, picked up the envelope and yelled behind Mae, "Fuck you Bitch! And don't come back, ever!" Then she rolled her eyes, walked inside the house, and slammed the door shut. Mae stepped into the taxi, closed the door and instructed the driver "Go."

They left South Carolina and settled in Virginia Beach for the longest period of time that they were on the run. Mae rented a room in a private house for them to live. They started boosting at a local department store called Tallheimer's. Tallheimer's was the Bloomingdale's of Virginia Beach at the time. Mae found some regular customers, but sometimes the connections to other customers would take them out to the housing projects in Norfolk, Virginia, which wasn't the safest of places to sell stolen goods. Mae went over there one day by herself to make a sale and was mugged on her way out of the projects. After that, Mae told Brenda never to go there by herself, because it could be a set-up.

Mae would eventually get busted at Tallheimer's. Of course, she already had a fancy lawyer in place who somehow knew how to get her off. Not long after that, Brenda also got busted at Tallheimer's. Mae contacted the lawyer to get Brenda out, and Mae paid the bail. But, Benda was ordered not to leave town and a hearing date was set for her. At the hearing, the very southern Judge referred to her as a 'slickster' from New York. He reminded Brenda that she violated her probation for charges in New York, and sentenced her to 1-5 years in jail. She ended up serving 12 months in the Norfolk City Jail. The Judge was going to send her back to New York to do her time, but she requested to do the time in Virginia so that when she went home to New York she would have a clean slate. She says she was just happy to be away from Mae, and living the way they were living. Mae bulked up Brenda's commissary account with about $2,000. Although she sent money, Mae would only visit Brenda twice in jail. The first time she came alone. At that visit she seemed distant, and Brenda knew something was up. The next time she came, she bought a man named Ray with her. Mae had met Ray through an acquaintance, and she had begun dating Ray while Brenda was in jail. Mae introduced Brenda to Ray and explained that she and Ray were soon-to-be married. She was very apologetic and couldn't really look Brenda in the eye. Ray seemed like a really nice man, and Brenda said she was happy because this was the best opportunity to get Mae out of her life for good. She wished them well, and she never saw Mae or Ray again.

Sobering

Although Brenda was in jail, she couldn't have felt freer. She had a lot of time to think, and she used it to think about her daughters, and sometimes she enjoyed not having to think about much of anything. She often turned to her first love, music. Her voice still sounded smooth and strong as she hummed and sang Zoom by the Commodores... 'I may be just a foooolish dreamer, but I don't caaaare. 'Cause I know my happiness is waiting out there, somewheeeeere.'

The jail was set up dormitory style, and her bunk had a window above it that looked out onto the Chesapeake Bay Bridge. Brenda thought a lot about her life, and while she was there, she studied and received her GED. She started to write letters to each of her girls, and would mail them all to Brooklyn. When Summer would visit on the weekend, Sabrina and Cheresse gave Summer her letters, and she would immediately tear them up without reading them. She was going into her junior year of High School, and refused to allow her to mess with her head. She had to remain focused on finishing high school, and figure out which college she was going to attend. Whatever Brenda wanted to say at that point was completely irrelevant to Summer.

Brenda turned to God and often consulted with the local priest who visited the jail. She told him about her life and how she had gotten to be where she was. She told him about her daughters back in New York, and how she was ashamed that she had left them. On Christmas the priest arranged for a care package of food to be sent to the apartment in Brooklyn on Brenda's behalf. It was a kind gesture from him, but Summer didn't care that it came from her. Her thinking was Brenda needed the food more than they did, and when she visited, she wouldn't eat any of it.

Brenda spent twelve months of her five-year sentence in Virginia. She was released early for good behavior and sent home on a one-way bus ticket financed by the priest. From Port Authority Bus Terminal, she took the A train to Brooklyn where Karla met her at the Grant Avenue train station. When she got off the train and saw Karla standing there, she was elated to see how beautiful her daughter was, but she also felt very ashamed. They walked the several blocks to the complex as Karla caught her up on gossip about the neighbors. It helped fill the space between them. It was strange to be back at this place, with all the neighbors knowing what had happened to her family, and to be back in

the apartment she had run away from three years earlier. Her daughters

were somehow able to hold onto the apartment, no thanks to her. Sabrina

and Cheresse greeted her with a hug, but didn't do a whole lot of talking

and sharing. It was not a family reunion as much as it was a mercy

offering. Brenda humbled herself just as she had practiced with the

priest, and was grateful to be camping out on the couch. Karla had

moved back to Brooklyn after she turned 18, leaving Summer in the

Bronx. Sabrina, Cheresse and Karla had their own rooms now, and they

were not about to give them up to accommodate Brenda, after all she had

put them through. She said she didn't mind taking any space that was

available, and that she was just glad to be home. Karla could not bear to

see her mother sleeping on the couch, and let her move into her room

with her after two weeks. Brenda quickly signed up for public assistance,

and welfare sent her to school to learn electronics. After completing the

program, she was able to get a job installing cable television with a

company called Manhattan Cable TV. By 1984, Brenda took on a second

job as a courier for DHL Courier Company.

In June of 1985, Summer graduated from high school, earning a

diploma and a New York State Cosmetology License. Dill had phoned

asking if he could attend the graduation ceremony. Everyone was shocked, especially Brenda. He had never taken an interest in her daughters before, so it was a strange request. But, he attended nonetheless. Jimmy, Brenda, Dill, and all of Summer's sisters attended the ceremony. It was a miracle to have the family all together all at once.

Summer was accepted to Hunter College and started classes in the Fall of 1985. Sabrina had moved out and shared an apartment in downtown Brooklyn with her friend Shandra. Cheresse was working full-time for Cynthia Woolridge, who had been a Councilwoman in the East New York section of Brooklyn for many years. Brenda reclaimed her bedroom, and started to have a steady stream of drunk and drug-addicted friends frequently visiting her. She lost her jobs, and was back on welfare. Cynthia worked out a deal to get Cheresse moved to the top of the waiting list for her own apartment in one of the buildings on the other side of the complex. While she was waiting for the paperwork to be processed, Cheresse put a strong lock on her bedroom door so she wouldn't come home one day and find she's been robbed. Summer had moved back into her old bedroom with Karla, but was determined to secure a dorm room at school. She'd spent every day of her first year of college harassing the Dean for a room, to which he'd repeatedly told her "Nothing yet," until one day he handed her the keys to her new room.

She packed her few things, and quickly moved into the dorm room at the start of Sophomore year.

Truth

Brenda had known Peaches since 1969, during her days living in Ozone Park. She was a very petite, light, brown-skinned woman with long, shiny black hair. Apparently, there was some kind of Cherokee Indian blood somewhere down the line in her family. She had given birth to three children, all of which were being cared for by her mother and other family members. So, she was an absent mother, unemployed and an active, practicing drug addict. The worst kind of influence Brenda could have had at such a crucial time of recovery in her life. The only slightly positive aspect to their relationship was that she was not physically abusive like Mae. Peaches started spending the night at the apartment, and after a while he just never left.

Summer went to see Brenda one afternoon. She rang the doorbell and a gaunt-looking man opened the door. She asked, "Is Brenda here, it's her daughter." He said nothing, and stepped aside to let her in. That putrid crack smell hit her. She could taste it entering her nostrils and lungs and she felt sick. The walls looked greasy and wet, and she avoided touching anything. She walked into the living room and saw

NOBODY'S CHILD: A BIOGRAPHY 291

two men sprawled across the crush velvet couch where she used to sit to eat bowls of cereal and watch cartoons on Saturday morning. The material was matted and what used to be a white couch was now dark gray. Summer was shocked a tv was still there. She continued walking back to her mother's room and knocked on the door. Brenda and Peaches had been getting high for days, and were in the middle of freebasing when Summer knocked on her bedroom door. She heard the door unlock, and a skeletal-framed, sallow-skinned Peaches cautiously opened the door. Then, someone who vaguely resembled her mother looked up from the drugs she was fixing, took a few seconds to focus and recognize who she was, "Hey, baby." Summer peeked in at the stranger, "I need to talk with you, in private." She got up from the bed, leaving the drugs laid out, and told Peaches to finish up. She pulled the door closed behind her. Peaches locked the door back. "Step into my office" Brenda said, and led Summer to the 'big' bathroom (not to be confused with the little bathroom, which had no tub, and was being used by someone smoking crack). Once inside with the door closed, Summer stared at this person in front of her and could not believe what she was seeing. Brenda, once a thick, full-breasted 38DD, with flawless brown skin and a beautiful smile now weighed less than 100 pounds, and her skin hung off of her bones. The once butter-soft brown skin on her face was almost charcoal colored and leather-like. Her teeth were yellow and brown, and they were chipped and spaced apart. She smelled like crack, liquor and despair. Brenda sat on the toilet seat, fidgeting, and jittery. She couldn't seem to focus her attention on one thing, looked everywhere but at Summer's face. Summer was looking around too, in this room where she used to shower and brush her teeth before school. Everything looked very dirty, and greasy, as if it hadn't been cleaned in at least a year. She remembered all the times her mother would raise hell at her and her sisters if chores weren't completed on Saturday mornings, and mourned for that tyrant who didn't live there anymore. She couldn't help but notice the red rubber, oddly-shaped water bag with the dingy white hose attachment that was draped on a wire hanger in the shower. She imagined one of the crackheads she passed in the living room caring enough about her hygiene to actually douche with it, and she wanted to vomit. She watched this stranger siting down on the toilet seat, crossing her legs, then uncrossing them, then crossing them again. She was nervous, and couldn't sit still. She didn't look at Summer in the face. Summer needed to get through this... "I've been seeing a therapist because I have a lot of angry feelings about things that happened in my life." No reaction. "The therapist said I should come and talk to you and tell you how I'm feeling, get it off my chest." She said she had been

harboring ill feelings toward her and Jimmy as a result of their life

decisions and how they had affected her. She said she didn't understand

why she lived the way she did, why she left her, why she wasn't there

for her and her sisters the way she should have been as their mother. In

the five minutes they spent in that bathroom, it seemed to take every

ounce of Brenda's strength to stay focused on what her daughter was

saying. She was looking everywhere but in Summer's eyes. Brenda's

face contorted as she tried to focus and process what her daughter was

saying. She was crossing and uncrossing her legs again, looking up at

her, then to the ceiling, then the floor and saying "uhh huh…. Uhh huh…

oh, oh…" Summer's heart was hardening and cracking from the inside

with each word bouncing off of her mother. She was not hearing or

understanding. Summer pressed on. She had to get the words out,

because she had to complete this task. She hurried. "Do you understand

what I'm saying, Ma?" Brenda furrowed her brows, scrunched her face

and concentrated hard, "Yeah, Yeah….. You got a dollar?" The words

broke Summer. The heat welled in her belly, and rose into her throat

until she couldn't speak. She looked at this shell of what used to be her

mother, and she wept for her, and wept for herself. "No, Ma. I don't have any money. I have to go now." She opened the bathroom door, and left her mother's apartment and never returned there again.

A Moment with Alice

One crisp Fall day in 1994, Brenda arrived for a visit at the Hill home in Hollis, NY. She greeted her younger sister Joy, and big sister Marilyn with kisses and hugs and they all shared a simple Sunday afternoon meal of baked chicken, white rice, mixed vegetables, cornbread, freshly brewed iced tea with lemon, and a store-bought lemon iced cake for dessert. Alice hadn't been baking much anymore, and was using a cane to ambulate around the house. Brenda noticed how much her mother had aged, but she was still one of the most beautiful, striking women she had ever seen. She was just grateful to be there, and wanted to enjoy the moment. She had missed so many moments like this when Dill was alive. He had passed away the previous summer. Brenda had mixed emotions about his death, and preferred not to talk about it.

Joy went down into the basement to warm up her voice and practice two new songs she would be performing in a few days with a world-renowned reggae funk band. Alice loved hearing her youngest daughter's melodic voice carried throughout the house. Marilyn had gone upstairs to put the finishing touches on one of her beautiful paintings. She had acquired a love of art honestly from her mother over the years, and currently worked as a framer for Barnette Gallery in Manhattan. It was a job she enjoyed, and was a one-off as she got to showcase her work when she had pieces to sell. Brenda opted to stay in the living room, just to be near her mother. She couldn't really get close enough physically to Alice without her being uneasy. Brenda had always attributed this to Dill's intimidation. Of course, it was a lot easier to blame him. She really didn't know what to think. She didn't want to give this rare moment over to Dill. She had Alice all to herself right now, and it felt wonderful. Brenda picked up her empty saucer with cake crumbs, and held the fork gently in place so that it didn't fall, or clank so as not to disturb Alice's focus on an intense game of Hollywood Squares on tv. She was seated in Dill's tan, brown and green upholstered Barcalounger. "Mom" she said softly from the kitchen, "you want anything else while I'm in here?" "No, thanks, Love" Alice replied sweetly. Brenda smiled a tiny smile. It felt good to hear her call her Love. When she came back into the living room, she sat on the floor and tucked her legs under her bottom, then she gently slipped her right hand under Alice's left hand on the chair's armrest. She waited for Alice to move her hand, but she didn't. They both stared straight as host Peter Marshall asked Paul Lynde a true or false question. "Mom, who was my real father?" Brenda slipped into the moment. Alice adjusted her right arm into the familiar ridge of fabric, a remnant of Dill's years of tv elbow. She pulled her right hand away, seemingly to adjust her body up and then back down into the chair. She was agitated, and this was upsetting her. Brenda watched as her eyes darted from the tv to the staircase going up to Marilyn's room then back to the tv again. She held her breath in hopes for an answer. She prayed her sisters wouldn't come in see Alice agitated and be mad at her. She just wanted the truth. "Why would you want to talk about old stuff? No one wants to talk about all that nonsense," Alice said. She didn't look at her daughter. Brenda couldn't say anything. She didn't mean to upset Alice, but she just thought now that Dill was gone, maybe, just maybe she would tell her the truth. Even in death, Dill still had a hold on her mother. Defeated, she braced herself, got up onto her feet, and excused herself down the hallway. She went into the bathroom, closed the door and cried 52 years of tears into the soft peach bath towel hanging on a hook behind the door.

Rock Bottom

*Brenda: Peaches was my friend. We had a lot of fun together.
But we were no good for one another… and, well, things started
going South.*

Crack cocaine has a metallic, putrid smell that penetrates the nostrils and

clothes when it comes into contact. It is a smell that's unforgettable.

In 1995, Brenda hit rock bottom. She had come into seriously

delinquent arrears with the management company at the apartment

complex, and had turned the apartment into a known crack den. The

management company had given her so many breaks over the years,

because everyone knew each other and their struggles. But, by now, they

had had enough of her. She woke up one day and an eviction notice was

posted on the apartment door, giving her thirty days to vacate. In true

Brenda fashion, she did what came naturally… she and Peaches

abandoned the apartment. Brenda had racked up thousands of dollars in

rent, and had no money to make any deals to stay. She was also in no

condition to navigate the public assistance system, going down to the welfare office, submitting necessary documentation, proving residency, etc. So, she packed the few things she considered valuable that she could carry, and left the rest for the crack addicts and salvage workers who were scheduled to clean the apartment out the next day. She lost heirlooms, valuable memorabilia, rare family photographs, her mother's jewelry, antique pieces of furniture, and vintage records, including the only copy of the song she recorded with Jimmy, 'You Ain't No Friend of Mine'.

Brenda and Peaches went to stay with Peaches' mother at her house in South Ozone Park, Queens. It was an old, two-story house in a quiet, residential neighborhood, the same neighborhood where Peaches and Brenda had met years earlier. The house was clean and kept up fairly well. But, it was in need of much repair and updating. The old wood floors creaked when the smallest child walked on them, and you could hear people talking in the kitchen even when you were on the top floor. It was a place to lay their heads for a while, but not a place to live. Peaches' mother, Mrs. Jenkins, had been caring for her young grandsons, since she was using drugs and in no position to care for children. Being back at her mom's gave Peaches a chance to spend time with her sons (and gave her mother hope that Peaches would actually have a chance to get clean). The primary rule in her house was absolutely 'NO DRUGS whatsoever'. She was a devout Christian, and would not stand for any foolishness, or else they would have to leave immediately. They both knew the rules, and would never disrespect Ms. Jenkins's home. The other rule was that Peaches would sleep downstairs in the basement, and Brenda would have to sleep upstairs in the smaller guest room, which was next to Ms. Jenkins's bedroom. Ms. Jenkins seemed to be pleased that her estranged daughter had come home, and she encouraged her to get off/stay off of drugs, if no other reason than to build a closer relationship with her sons. Brenda made a deal with Ms. Jenkins that she would do what she had always been taught to do, keep the house clean, fix things that were broken around the house, and grounds-keeping. In return, she would have a place to rest her head and food to eat. Brenda was grateful for the compromise. She figured it was better than being homeless.

That same summer, Sabrina married her long-time boyfriend Gregory in a beautiful ceremony at St. Albans Congregational Church, and the reception was held at the lovely Queens Botanic Gardens. It completely broke Sabrina's heart that her mother, who Sabrina could not find, was not there to see her get married. Thankfully, Jimmy was present and happy to give his eldest daughter away to her love. In August of that same year she gave birth to a baby girl. With joy sometimes comes pain.

Kate passed away only three days after Sabrina's wedding. The wedding

invitations had been sent out months earlier, and Kate kept insisting that

she didn't believe she would be able to make the trip from Pennsylvania,

where she and Dave had moved years earlier. Sabrina kept telling her

she would travel to get her, or send for her. She just couldn't see herself

getting married without Kate being there. But, Kate kept putting her off.

Dave had passed away in 1983, and since then Kate lived alone in the

downstairs apartment of the three-story home owned by her sister Joanie.

Joanie's husband also died some years earlier. Sabrina, along with

Cheresse and Summer were all devastated at the loss of their beloved

Nana. And, it felt like a tragedy that she would never get to meet her

great-granddaughter. She would have loved being a great-grandma.

Sabrina and Gregory were forced to use their wedding gift money to help

pay for Kate's funeral arrangements, and to get her personal affairs in

order. Although she had made some plans for her death, there was still

$6,000 in expenses that needed to be taken care of. Her granddaughters

traveled to Norristown, Pennsylvania for the funeral. They had to pool

their money to cover the expenses.

Brenda had barely cleaned herself up just long enough to somehow get herself to Pennsylvania for the services. She arrived high, playing the good daughter role. She had no money to help with expenses, she was in no condition physically to assist with cleaning up. The thing she was most interested in was fishing through Kate's jewelry, or trying to identify any cash that Kate may have left behind. She was only permitted to take a few photos, and one ring of her mother's. Otherwise, she was shut out of that part of the grieving process, and she resented her daughters for it. She felt somehow entitled. She wanted an inheritance, and she was looking for respect... not just from her daughters, but also from cousins, aunts, uncles and neighbors she hadn't seen since she was a very young girl. It wasn't the reception she was hoping for, because no one wanted to chat about old times with a crackhead. They felt embarrassed for Brenda, and mourned for Kate who would be mortified at what her daughter had become. Brenda left the house and got lost for a while. She walked a few blocks away to a local bar and finagled a few drinks out of people who offered their condolences. It was easier to go out and have a drink with strangers than spend hours under the watchful eyes of her judgmental daughters. They stayed up and shared memories about how funny and sweet Kate was, and how she was such a feisty, peppy little lady. The funeral was held at Kate's small church where she had been a member since she had been back in Norristown. It was very disturbing that the body in the casket didn't look anything like Kate. In life, she was a fair-skinned woman with freckles all over her face, a beautiful smile and warm complexion. In death, she was bloated, and her face was covered in a dark pancake make-up (far from her own natural skin color). She looked so unlike herself that it was as if they were attending the funeral of a stranger. Summer accepted one of the programs prepared by the staff at the church, looked down at a picture on the front, and felt better that it was a much better likeness of Kate's real face. They all took their seats in the appropriate pew. Brenda was very emotional, crying and performing for Kate's friends, family members, and the congregation. She played on their sympathies the way drug addicts do. It was the most attention she had received in a long time and she was going to make the most of the moment. She was grieving the death of her mother, whom she had not seen or spoken with in many years. But, she also saw an opportunity to establish a few contacts who she could manipulate and possibly use later on. The pastor and missionaries had worshipped and volunteered alongside Kate, and they knew her well. They spoke highly of her, and the pastor said beautiful things about the kind of life she led.

Darkest Before Daylight

Peaches started dating a man she knew from high school named Junior. He had always been interested in her, but never approached her. He ran into her while picking up her eldest son from school one day. He dropped Peaches off at the house and stopped in to say hello to Ms. Jenkins, who he hadn't seen in many years. She probed him for a while, asking whether he was married, had kids, and what he did for a living. He explained he had been working with Con Edison for seven years, had no children and was single. He also attended church nearby. Junior started staying for dinner, and not long after he had moved into the basement with Peaches and the kids. Brenda, who had always been friends with Peaches, was jealous but did not have any place else to go. So, for four months she tried to ignore Peaches and Junior, take care of her chores, and disappear as often as possible. She wandered mostly, trying to score some drugs. One morning before Brenda could leave the house, Ms. Jenkins told her to sit down in the living room. She said she appreciated the job Brenda was doing with helping out around the house and fixing things. However, she told her it was time for her to move on.

She had to find another place to stay. She explained it wasn't approp[

for her to stay any longer now that Peaches had moved on. She told[

it would be better for Peaches, and the boys if Brenda left. She w[

giving her one week to find another place to live. She wasn't mean about

it. She actually liked Brenda a lot as a person. But, she was a mess, and

she was an adult who needed to get her life in order. It was time for

Brenda to figure out what she was going to do next.

On a warm evening in late May, 1995, Brenda was walking back to

the Jenkins home in Ozone Park. At 2am she had called it quits after

partying with two friends she hadn't seen since her days at Bruer Bar.

There was plenty of crack and weed to go around, so she was very high

when she walked out into the warm night air up on Rockaway Boulevard.

The street was as busy as it always was at that time of morning on a

Friday, with cars whirring by every 20 seconds or so. A few people who

passed her on the sidewalk could see she was a bit unsteady on her feet,

and graciously adjusted their path to accommodate her. She was grateful

and kept walking. She was deep in thought trying to figure out what her

next move was going to be. Ms. Jenkins had given her one week to find

another place to live, and she had exhausted all of her go-to's for cash,

or places to crash. She had to figure out what to do next. Kate was gone.

was gone. Her daughters were doing ok, but she refused to burden

ever again. She would figure it out on her own, she always did.

Brenda hadn't noticed the man in the blue van pull up near the bus

op. As she walked past, he leaned over to roll down the passenger

window and said, "Hey, you wanna party?" She slowed down her pace

to try to focus and see who it was. He didn't look familiar, but she was

trying hard to focus on his face inside the dark van. The moonlight only

revealed he was a dark-skinned, older black man, short beard and

mustache, and an army green military cap. "I got drugs," he said in a

slightly lower tone. Brenda was already high enough, but she didn't want

to turn down the chance to get a little bit more. She didn't know when

she would score again the way things were going. She stumbled up into

the passenger seat and they drove off. He told her his name was Curtis,

and he lived just a few blocks up and they could party all night. She

knew this neighborhood like the back of her hand. She had raised her

girls there, and all her friends from 147th Street still lived there. She

tried to think about when life was much simpler, but it only made her

ashamed and she wanted to forget all of that right now. She wondered

how close Curtis lived. He made a right down 143rd Street, left on

130th... or was it a right? He made a quick left into the dead-end street

on 144th. He made a three-point turn and backed the van up into the driveway until the van's bumper pushed against the garage door. He

her they were there and to come inside. She stepped down from

passenger side and followed him to the garage. He turned the doorkn

opened the door and flipped on the lights. She thought they would wal

through the garage and go into the connected house. But, before she

could turn to ask him where to go she felt a MACK truck hit her on the

right side of her skull (at least if felt like a truck). Blood gushed from

her head, she felt dizzy and fell to the floor, a concrete slab floor that was

cold and grainy with dirt. She held her head and tried to speak but it was

too late. Curtis was pulling her thin body out of her jacket, her shirt, her

pants, her socks, her sneakers, her underwear, her bra. He threw her

clothes to the side, turned her over on her knees and entered her hard,

pulling and pushing with all his weight, scraping her knees across the

floor, tearing her flesh. She tried to scream, but he punched her in the

back and head warning her to "shut up". She was still so out of it from

earlier. She didn't have much fight in her. Now he was on top and

entering her from behind with such a force it felt as if her spine was going

to crack. She couldn't speak, so she prayed for God to help her. She

cried as she felt her breast, shoulders and stomach bleed and burn from

the scraping. Finally, after what felt like forever, he grunted hard and

e. She was in excruciating pain, cold, sore, ashamed, and grateful it

over. She felt paralyzed, unable to bend her knees or push her upper

dy up with her hands. So, she laid there, unsure how long. It was

itch black and Curtis had disappeared. She felt around for her clothes,

but she could not find them. She felt wet between her legs, she was

bleeding and wanted to at least use her shirt or pants to wipe her body

off, then put them on to get warm, and get out of there. She bumped

around in the garage feeling the walls, floor, door... she found the door.

She turned the knob but it was locked and felt bolted shut. She banged

on the door, but no one answered. She tried lifting the garage door, but

it wouldn't budge. She now realized why he had bumped the van up

against it. Motherfucker, she thought. She sunk down to the floor and

tried to figure out what to do. Brenda could see daylight from underneath

the door, so she knew she had been there for at least ten hours. Every

hour or so, she would get up, bang on the door, scream, nothing. She

was starving, freezing cold, and in desperate need of a hit. Was he

coming back? Had he planned to kill her? Was this going to be how she

finally dies? Will her daughters finally get a call saying her body was

found in some garage? She shuddered at the thought of what that would

do to her poor family.

She was awakened by the sound of a bolt being removed and the

opening. She could see it was nighttime again. Then the door cl(

and locked. She cowered in the corner but felt a hand yank her forwa

throwing her down hard onto the floor again. He continued to rape h(

repeatedly for hours, entering nearly every orifice in her body, doing

unspeakable things, then leaving again, with no food, no water, no

clothes. On day three, she heard the bolt unlock, a car door slam, an

engine start, then she heard the garage door give and relax as he drove

away. She had to use every ounce of energy she could muster to pull her

battered body over to the door. She prayed the knob would turn. It did.

She opened the door to sunlight. She peeked out and saw nothing and

no one. She looked back into the garage and saw her clothes strewn on

the floor. She was weak, and in too much pain to try cleaning herself up.

She pulled her clothes on slowly, carefully... panties, shirt, pants, socks,

shoes, jacket, and shoved the bra into her coat pocket. She limped out

of the garage, and confirmed she was at the last house in the dead end of

144th Street (she remembered that). She had walked past that block so

many times over the years. Who would have thought I'd be here? She

thought about her daughters, she thought about Jimmy, she thought about and Dave, and Joanne and Donna, and even Mae. Most of all she

ght about Dill and Alice.

Ready!

Brenda did not go back to the Jenkins' right away. She walked around the neighborhood for four days, sleeping in doorways, scrounging for food behind Garcia's Deli, the Chinese restaurant, and the Rockaway Fish House. She acquired clothing, more each day, from business owners that knew her. It was 80 degrees, but she was going through withdrawals and couldn't get warmed up no matter how many layers. She wanted to die. She was exhausted and had all but given up. As she made her way down Inwood Street in the hot sun, she began rehearsing how she would explain where she had been for the past week, and why she had a busted lip and black eye. She had barely noticed the 1994 green Mercedes parked in front of Ms. Jackson's house. Sabrina stepped out from the driver's seat, closed the door and waited for Brenda to reach her. She stared at her mother, squinted her eyes from the sun, "Ma???" She knew it was Brenda, even under all the layers of clothing. She stood stoic. But, could not mask the agonizing sadness she felt at that moment for her mother. Brenda squinted with her healthy eye, then her dry lips ed a smile, a tiny tear where it had been trying to heal. She didn't

. Finally realizing "Sabrina??!!" she replied softly, voice hoarse,

oat dry. Sabrina didn't hesitate… she pulled her mother close to her

ıd squeezed her tightly. She smelled awful, but it didn't matter to either

ıne of them. Brenda squeezed tighter and whispered, "I'm ready to come

home."

> *Brenda: It was the worst time of my life. But, that was the best day of my life. Sabrina saved me. I got into that car with her and she drove me to Horizon Rehabilitation program. It was a long road after that, but I've stayed clean ever since. I still have a lot of work to do, but I'm on my way. (Standing now, she grabbed her jacket and bag, then heading for the door, the doctor following to see her off).*

> *Juwayriah: You're a remarkable woman, Brenda. I'm so glad we met. You should be very proud of yourself.*

> *Brenda: (turning back to the doctor and extending her hand) I am… she said (sounding happy and solemn at the same time). "There's so much more that happened after that, and I just wish we had the chance to talk more. I dread starting over with a new doctor in Georgia is all."*

> *Juwayriah: Brenda, the work never ends. You are a work in progress. We ALL are. You deserve a chance at happiness. Forgive yourself. Go be with your daughters… and your new grandchildren! (Whispering) Go live your life.*

> *Brenda: (with an air of newfound confidence) "I will." And she truly meant it.*

Brenda stepped out of the brownstone and into the bright, chill of the after rain. She could smell the rain drying out of the air, and moisture from the leaves on the trees. She thought about Dave.

To her surprise, she saw her beautiful family waiting at the curb, and watched the taxi she reserved drive away. Tyler stopped making funny faces at her puppy Mr. Whispers when she saw Brenda. "Grandma!" she giggled then bolted up the stairs two at a time, the lavender satin sash on her party dress swishing back and forth behind her. "I'll help you down Grandma," taking her hand and leading. Brenda was perfectly able to do it alone, but loved to let Ty have her way. She patted the top of her perfectly parted, pony-tailed head, and gave Ty her left hand. Her daughters looked on chuckling at the sight. "Ma, you good?" Cheresse asked. "I'm good baby" Brenda assured her. Satisfied, Cheresse walked around to the driver's side of her SUV and slid behind the wheel. Summer tucked the soft, yellow baby blanket under her son's neck to reveal his face and placed him gently into Brenda's arms. "Theeeeere's Grandma's baby," Brenda snuggled into the sleeping baby's ear. Summer got into the front passenger seat, while Karla helped her mother and nephew Christopher inside. Sabrina waited for her daughter to settle in beside Brenda, then reached over to fasten Ty's belt. "Thank you, nmy," she smiled. "You're welcome Ty" kissing her forehead. Mr.

ispers hopped into the third row and Karla climbed in after.

verybody ready?" Karla asked then shut the door behind her.

Ready!!!" Tyler shouted louder than everyone.

ABOUT THE AUTHOR

Tammie Francisque was born and raised in New York City. As the youngest of four, Tammie benefited greatly from observing the life experiences of the women in her life, especially her mother and three sisters. The earliest life-changing event she recalls is the divorce of her parents. At eight years old, Tammie and her sisters were uprooted from their home in Queens, and dropped into a new, more urban experience in Brooklyn. One year later, a stranger enters their lives and wreaks havoc on a once tight-knit family, turning their world upside down.

In a turbulent environment, Tammie grew up quickly and learned to fend for herself in many ways. Images of womanhood, motherhood and self-empowerment were being shaped in her mind, and with that she made the conscious decision to take responsibility for shaping her own future.

In 2002 Tammie met and fell in love with her husband William. He had grown up in a large, close-knit family with customs that were different from her own. He also wanted to be a father, and believed Tammie would be an excellent mother. It was the first time she had entertained being a parent. The sacrifices she needed and wanted to make for her child strengthened her, and created a purpose and pure joy she didn't realize she craved. More than at any other point in her life, Tammie wanted to share her maternal experience with her own mother.   Through cathartic interviews, Tammie learned her mother

experienced much during their years together and even more so in their

apart.   Nobody's Child: A Biography is a culmination of those emoti

interviews. Tammie's hope is that her Mother's wish to share her story with

world will give someone hope, and empower them to believe they can f

adversity and still be victorious.

This book is dedicated to ALL the children who felt disconnected, unlovec

and unwanted. It's for the children who had to grow up quickly, formulate a

plan, and push through despite the odds.

Tammie Francisque lives in New York with her family. This is her first

published work.